Itinerant Dreamer

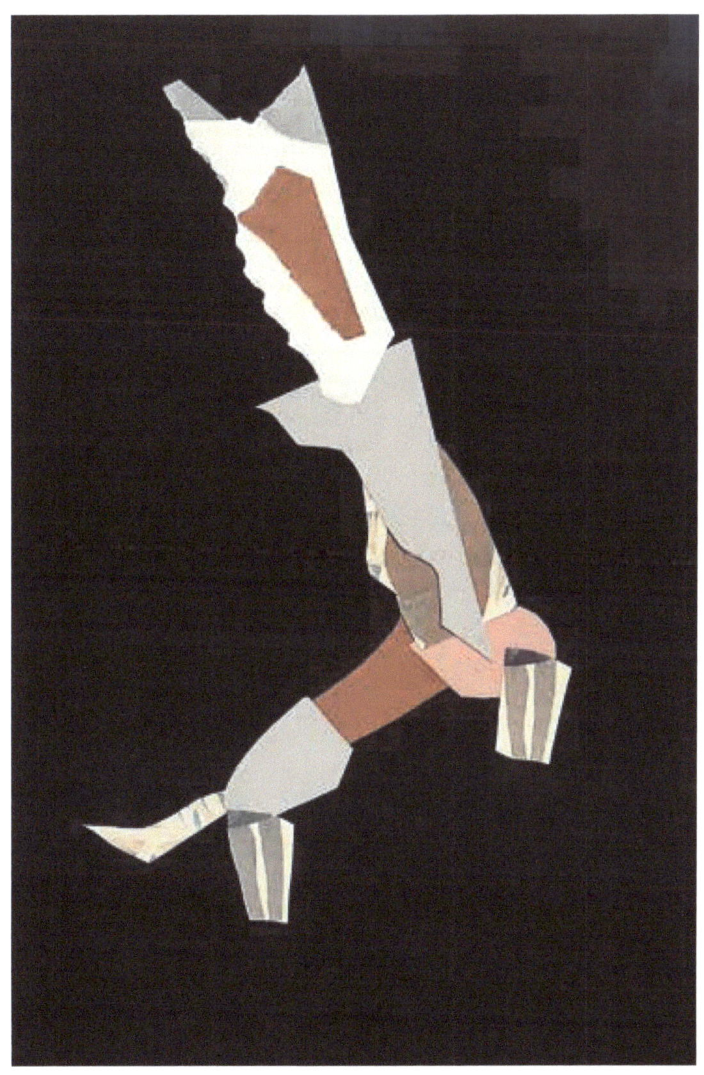

Doren Robbins

Itinerant Dreamer

Doren Robbins

Cover art by Doren Robbins
Cover art title: Rocking horse archetype

Published by Sandy Press (sandy-press.com)

ISBN-13: 979-8-9924582-1-3

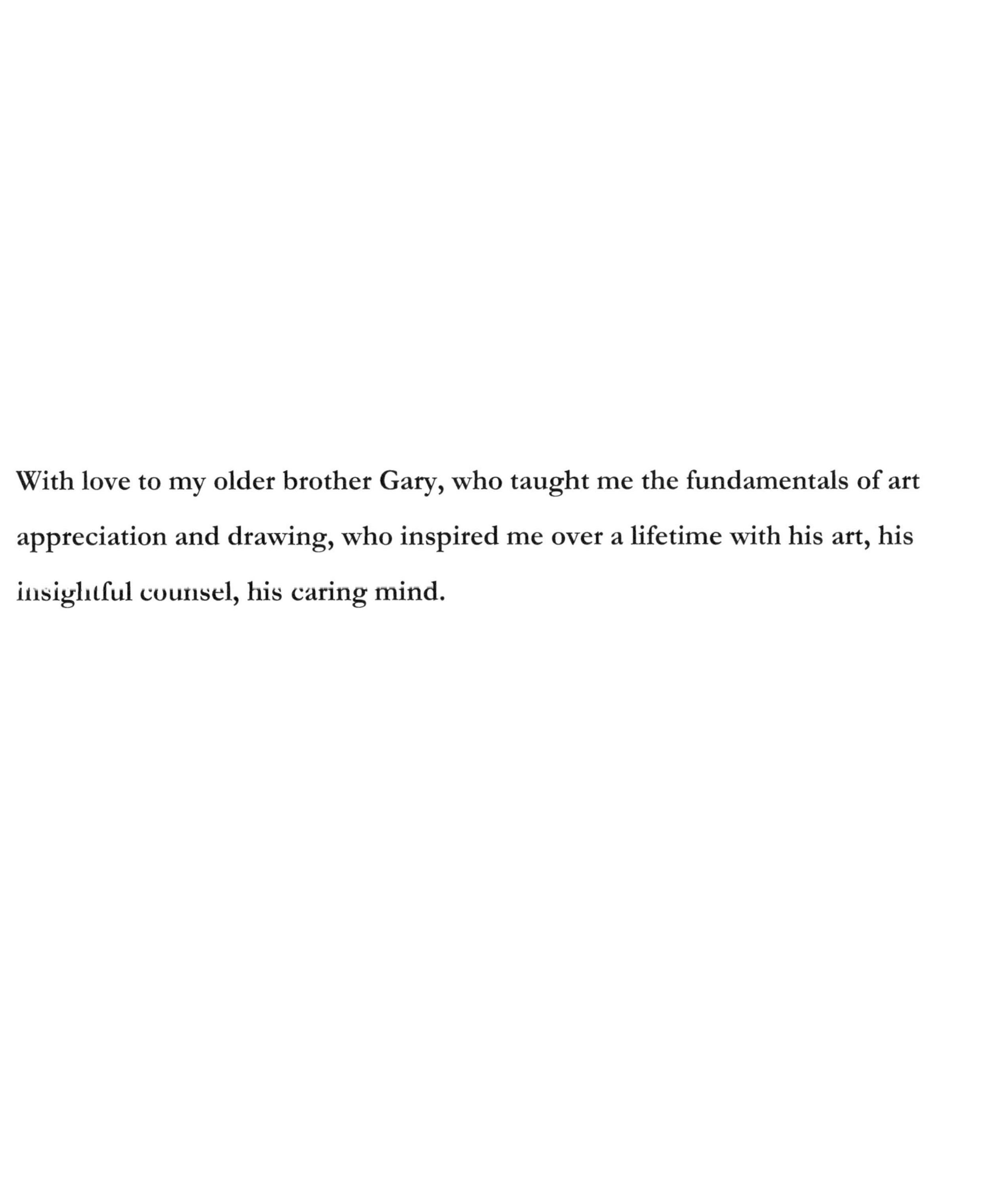

With love to my older brother Gary, who taught me the fundamentals of art appreciation and drawing, who inspired me over a lifetime with his art, his insightful counsel, his caring mind.

Table of Contents

Introduction

Mixed Media (And a Latent Un-Titled Unanswerable Message)

Intrigue is magnetic. Bewitching. Seductive. Mysterious. It's what makes intrigue intriguing. You never know what you're going to discover. It might be a drama on the radio that snares your attention. It might be a conversation overheard on the bus. A scream at the zoo, a mark on a wall, or a provocatively titled YouTube video. Within the purview of Robbins's *Itinerant Dreamer*, it might be nine heads, four wheel-locks, bottom tray, and a shopping cart, a collage rendered in ink, acrylic, and paper cut-outs. The mind immediately explodes into catechism: why this constellation of crudely rendered faces interspersed among grocery carts and wheel-locks? Why grocery carts? What is the significance of grocery carts? Why are the wheel-locks interspersed among the faces, which combine the dreamlike, inchoate tenor of primal impressions in a hectic dialectic, rendered with the raw expressiveness of art brut, à la Jean Dubuffet?

There are no definitive answers to these questions. The intrigue is in the artistry, the array of associations provoked into a contemplative juggling of narratives and explanations. None of which really matters. Rational explanation is not the end goal. It's the intrigue, the contrast between faces and carts, the grid-like background on which the faces and wheel-locks are constellated. Materials haven't been recruited for their appropriateness, but for their singular charms in a universe of chaos. In science, chaos theory describes systems where small changes in initial conditions can lead to large, unpredictable outcomes, like a puck in a hockey game, or the chatter of birdsong in a tropical forest, any insignificant event that might gain non-linear momentum and culminate in a coup in another hemisphere, or a UFO in Uruguay. Which, of course, is precisely what happens in a grocery store: the infinite miscellany of products, canned goods, fruit, cereals, frozen pies and pizzas and so on, not to mention the many faces of the clerks and shoppers, some gloomy, some locked in dour concentration, some in happy conversation, some vacant and unexpressive, consumed with the tedium of shopping, function as a collage in constant movement, everything from hummus to cornflakes to astronauts trapped in space.

Collage is what made surrealism so compelling. The completely irrational juxtaposition of images, some familiar, some strange, presented within a medium of paper and paint or wire and clay. Collage, however, was not strictly a surrealist invention; it first appeared among the Cubists when artists such as Braque and Picasso began incorporating actual objects in their painting.

Among the first of these is Picasso's *Still Life With Chair Caning*, which is considered to be modern art's first collage, in which he includes a section of actual wicker chair caning glued to the surface of the work, and Braque's *Fruit Dish and Glass*, in which he added wallpaper to the charcoal and gouache to the composition. The addition of such materials helps connect an artistic production with the actualities of contemporary life.

This is Robbins's wheelhouse: life. Life as it's being lived. Life as it employs an artistry of contrast and seeming incongruity to lift itself into a sphere of transcendent awareness. Connect the dots, so to speak. Combine the tragic with the sublime, the earthbound with the divine. "Man facing homeless camp," is a portrait of anguish. The face appears ghostly at first, a phantom being in a dying society, until you look closer and see the pain, the penciled sadness of an ongoing catastrophe. The shading around the eyes is bedrock haggard, and the eyes themselves have an uncanny lucidity. The torso is broad and is covered with undulating lines. There's a fullness to this figure, a bold acceptance of pain which is fully capable of treasuring moments of pleasure. It's spirit of indomitable humanity runs through this collection, a full spectrum of the macabre, the tragic, the harlequin, the intensity of love, the veneration of shape and line combined with the spectral vibrations of an underlying elsewhere.

"Man facing homeless camp" is followed by a poem. The poem, says Robbins, "plays out of Allen Ginsberg's poem, "Under the World There's a Lot of Ass," from *Mind Breaths*. Here, once again, we find shopping carts: "Under the world's leadership there's a lot of shopping carts." The line reads like a microcosm of a planet engulfed in corporate cupidity, a crisis of disequilibrium and late-stage capitalism. "under the world's leadership there's a lot of Haitians eating cookies held together with dirt," the poem continues, "an unbearable victims' aura to multiple races, unmovable bowel crust and toxic meat syndrome, Asshat media pundits surplus, hoppity rapidly following hippity, workers constructing Dracula's athletic shoes..."

It's a long poem, and reads as if it'd been fueled with high octane polychromatic wrath. The words flow fast, stumbling over one another in a brawling indemnification of a world overtaken by greed, war and corruption, a "Blackwater Felugia My Lai Bailout broth with the bones inside of it, with the purse inside of it, with the child's nose inside of it."

The bulk of material in this collection consists of Cubist-like collages and drawings, but there's a significant inclusion of Robbins's poetry. The writing, not surprisingly, shares the same mood and aesthetic as the artwork, but it does differ in some interesting ways.

The poems and prose (there are also essays) have the roughness and porosity of limestone. They comprise a landscape of bizarre contortions and a sinewy syntax aroused by a surge of urgency to contractions of socioeconomic tyranny. Robbins's essay on what he calls his "Iron Heel Sequence," bears an uncanny pertinence to our current constitutional crisis:

> The current agencies of The Iron Heel have become pervasive and incidental, cooperative when necessary, using violence, repression of civil liberties, and torture exercised internationally to maintain the Iron Heel's Totalitarian and Oligarchic global powers. Economic systems have become arbitrary to the corporate synthesis of international high finance. George Orwell represented the situation in the "War is Peace" passage of 1984: "All of the disputed territories contain valuable minerals…above all they contain a bottomless reserve of labor…reduced more or less openly to the status of slaves" (187). What Orwell understands through observation as the economic maintenance of The Iron heel Oligarchy, reflects Randolph Bourne's statement, "But in general, the nation in wartime attains a uniformity of feeling, a hierarchy of values, culminated at the undisputed apex of the State ideal, which could not possibly be produced through any other agency than war's" (Bourne).

Robbins's poetry is equally unflinching. The words have the consistency of blackberries, they're tart and sweet simultaneously, and surrounded by thorns, the complications of life in a single moment, a containing support, a framework, a proposition, a sudden stark observation. like a soup spoon holding a bone. "Listen," says Robbins,

> It took until the seventeenth century to paint dirt, plain farm dirt on the pads of a woman's feet seen from behind tucked underneath her while she handles red cow udders, and the man, his absolute distraction, this embodiment of a man possibly deranged in unfulfilled anticipations, a type of man possibly hostile over ending up in this painting perpetually waiting for milk or fingers and udders symbolic of something else latent in space, the latent un-titled unanswerable message and what brought this out of him.

- John Olson

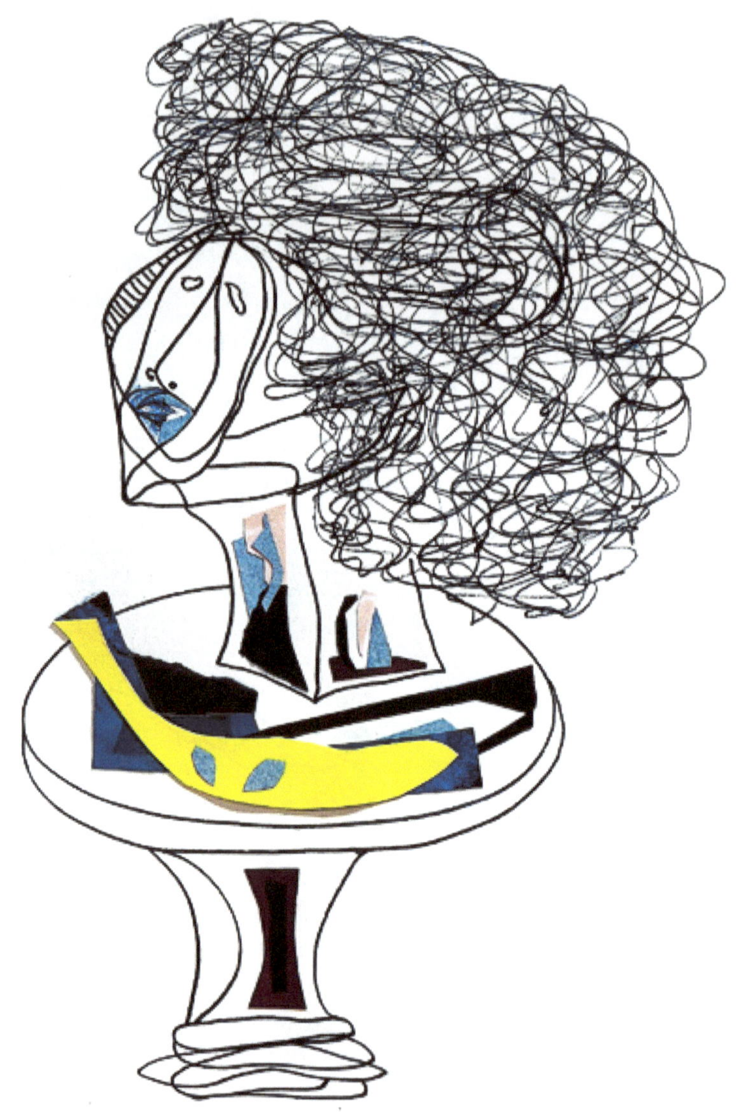

Uncomfortable with still life. Ink pen and cut-outs. 2017.

Introspection Series One

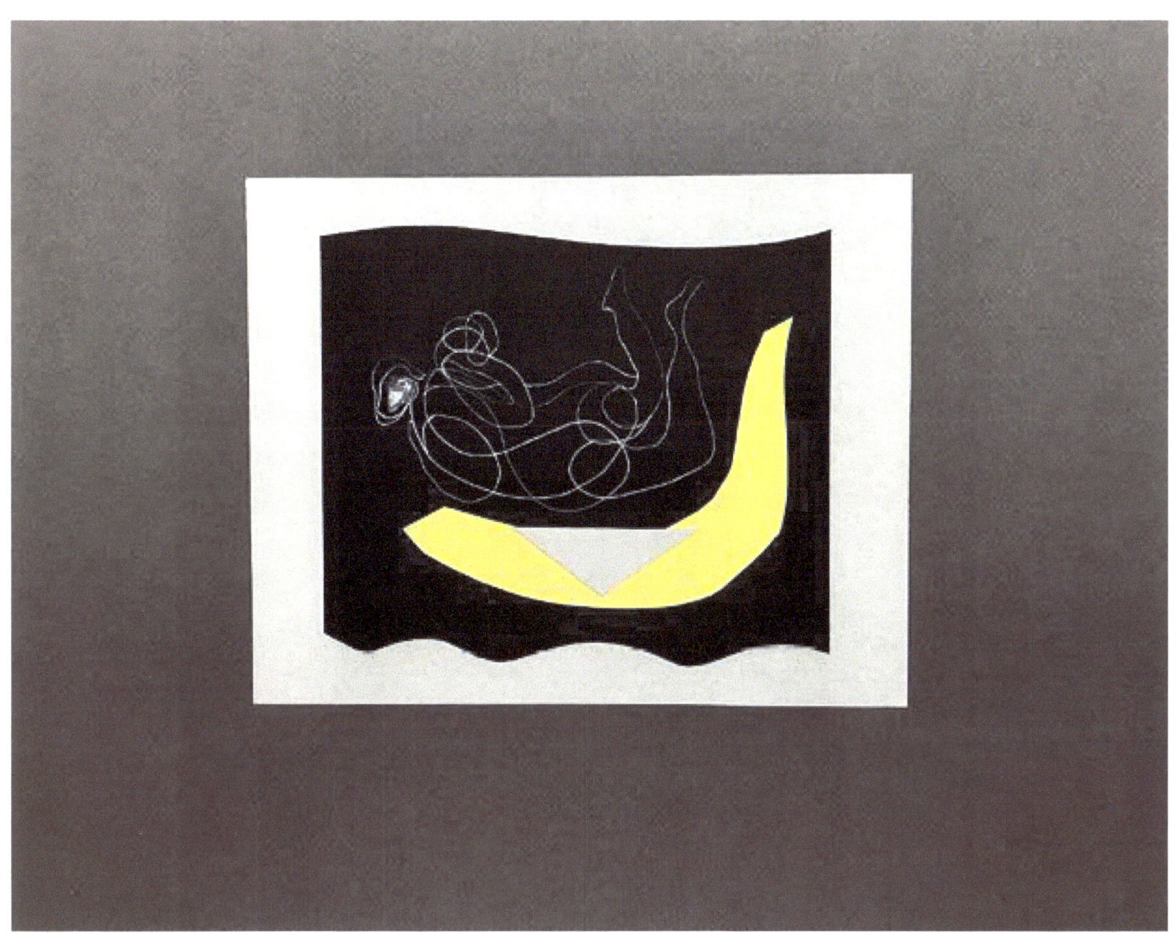

Itinerant Dreamer. Ink, acrylic, and cut-outs. 2022.

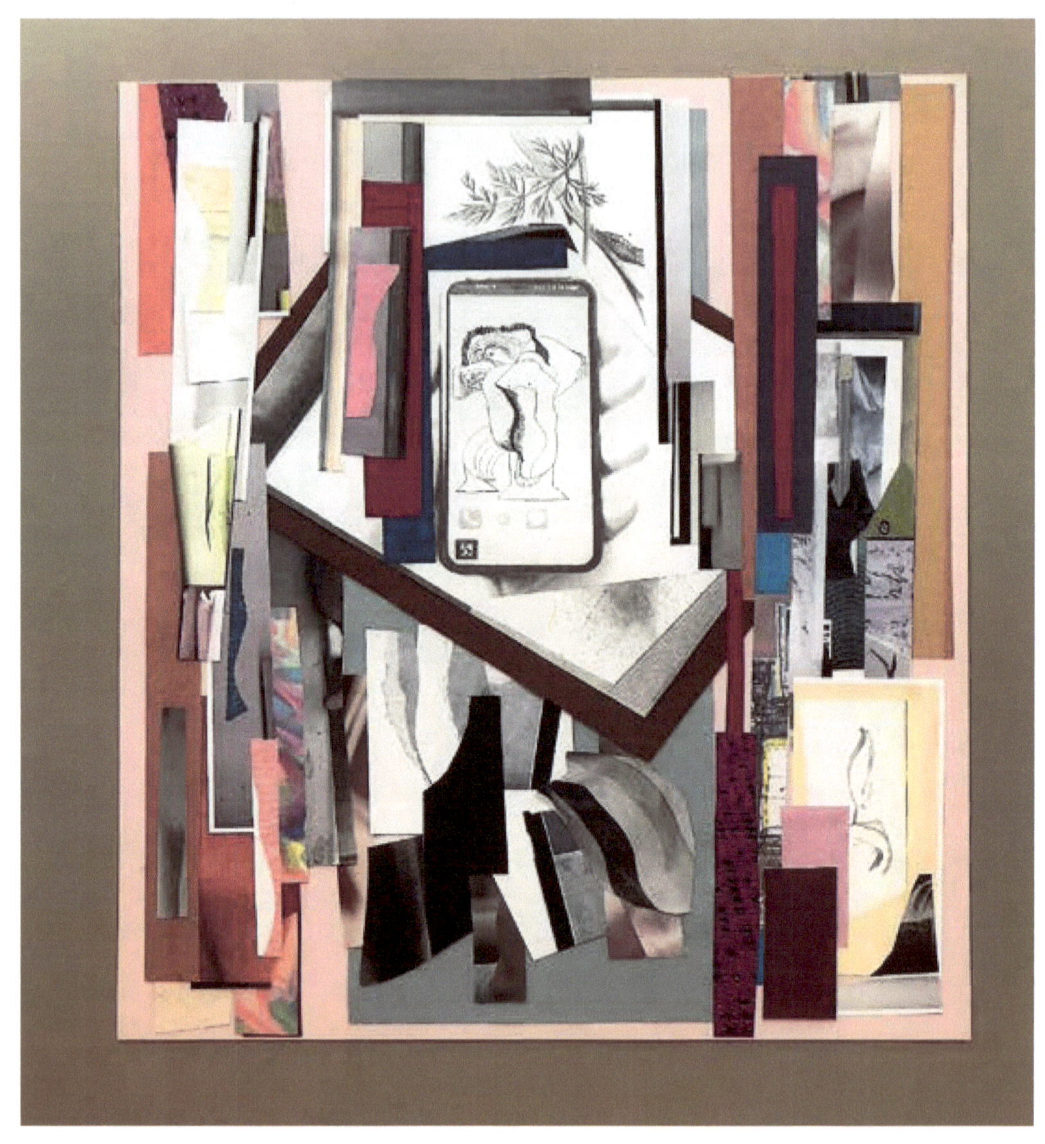

Unnamed, on table. 1987, 2013, 2017. Ink, watercolor, photomontage, collage.

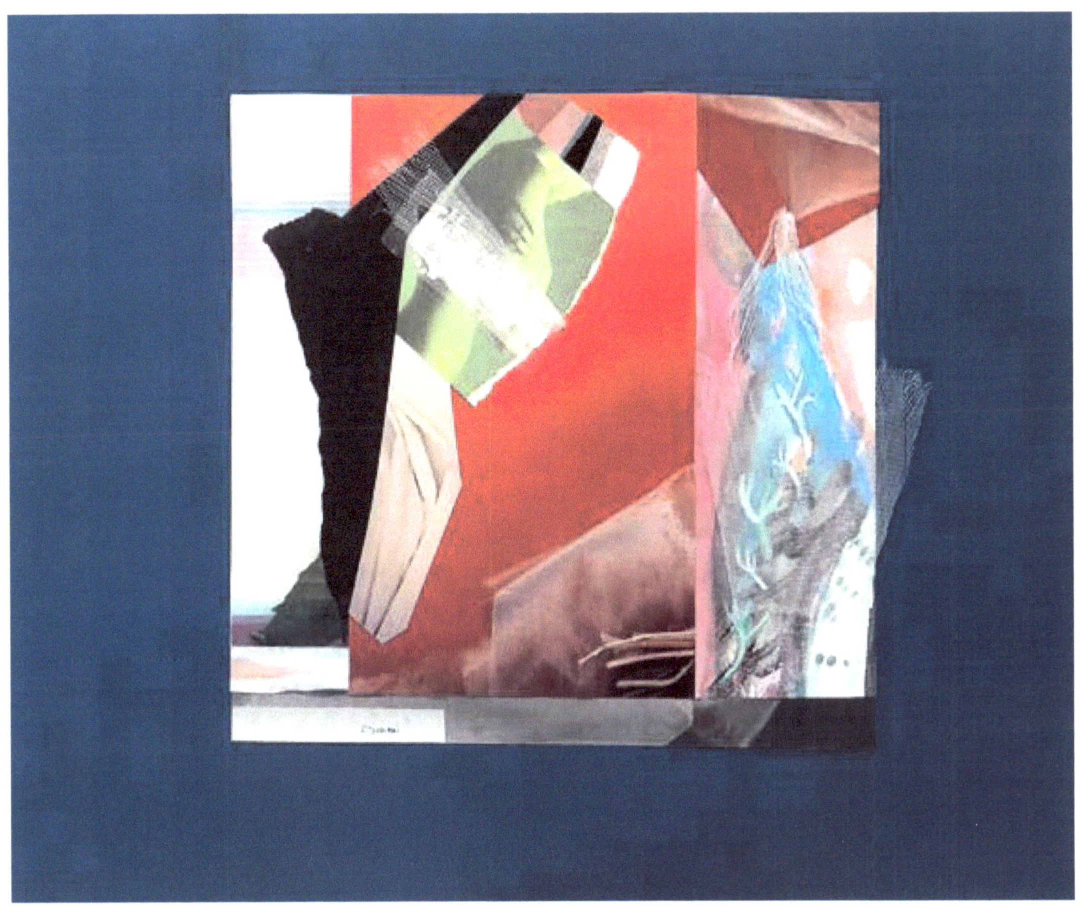

Introspection series-1C4. Watercolor, photomontage, and fabric. 2013.

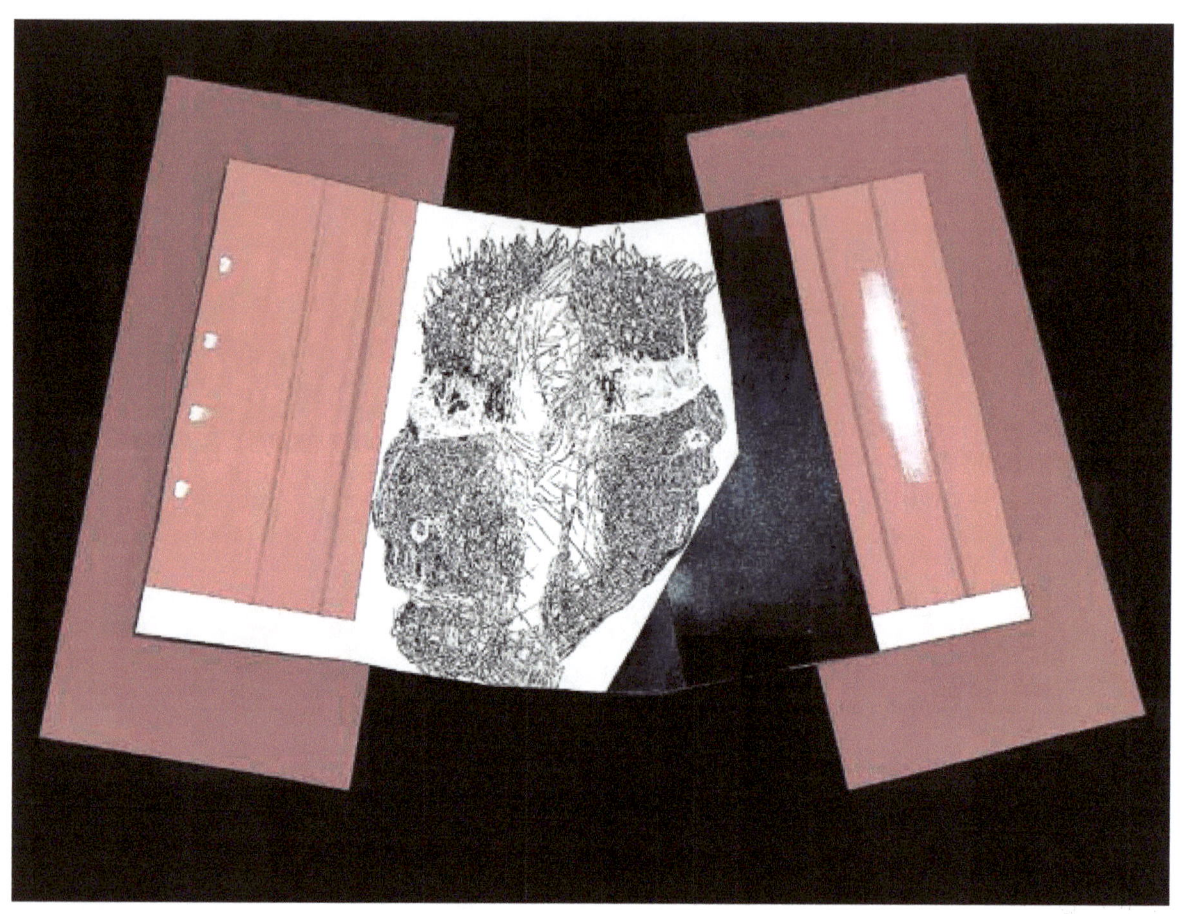

Theater. Ink, cut-out, constructed shred. 2015.

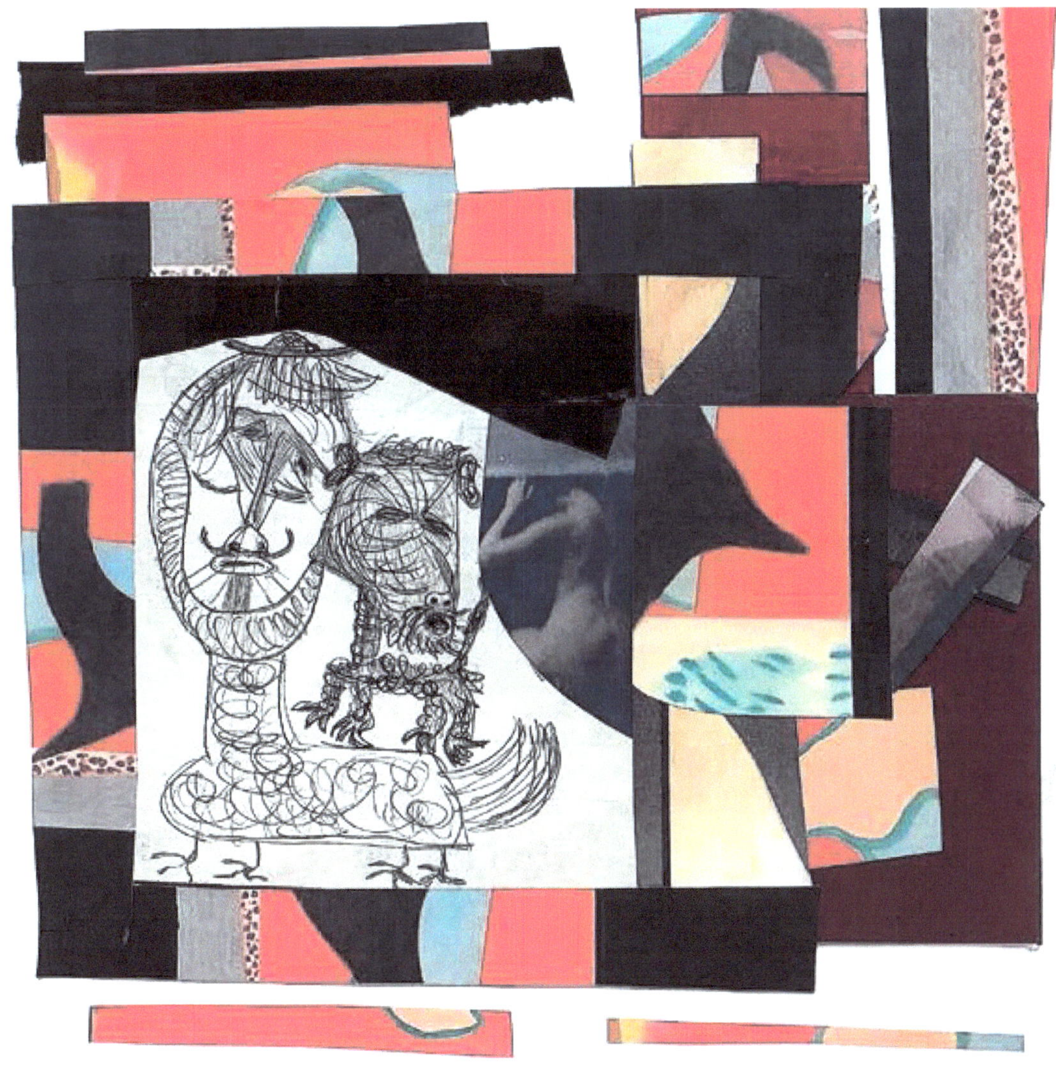

Don Quixote and Sancho Panza visit one of the Pleiades. Ink, graphite, watercolor, and photomontage. 1980, 2015.

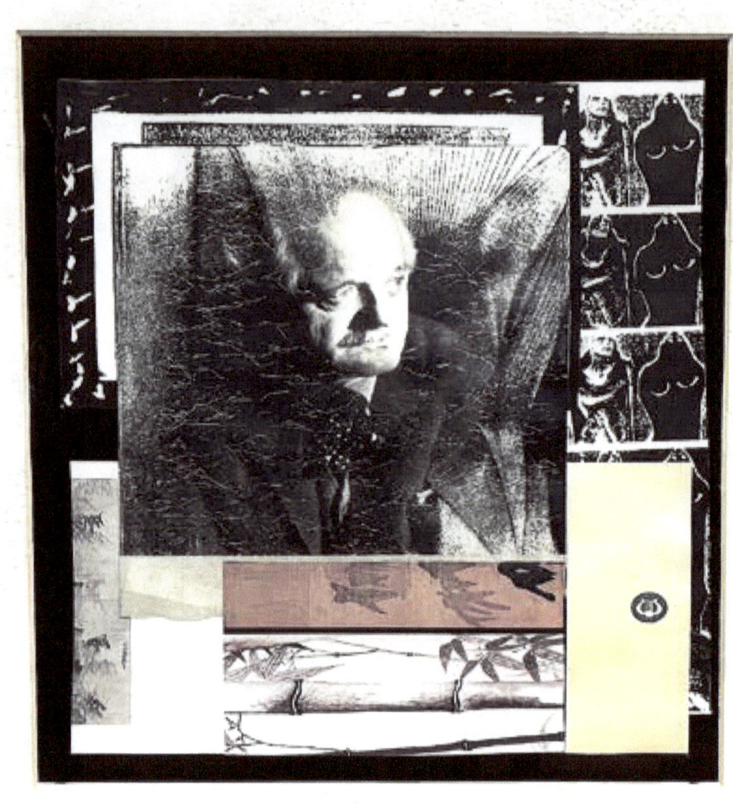

Rexroth now. Resurfaced photo, collage, and ink. 1999, 2006.

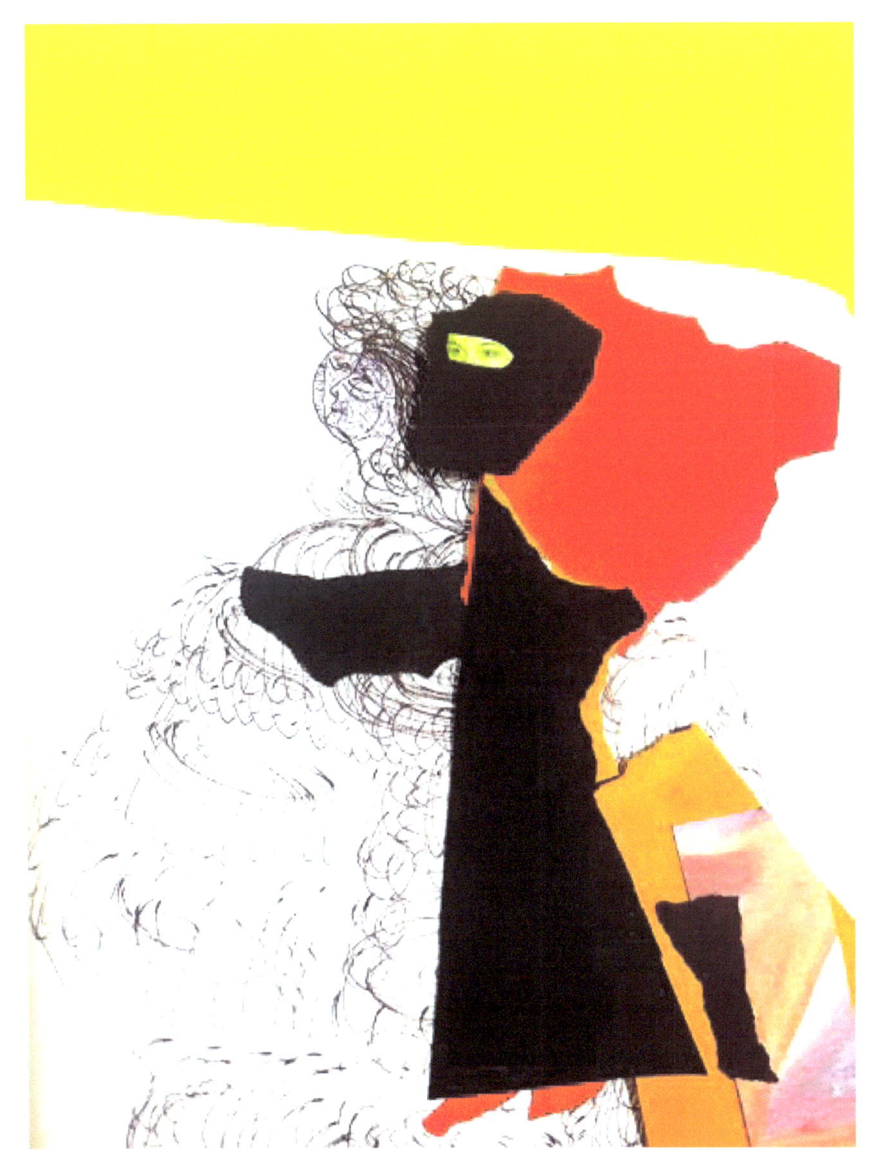

Visitors. Ink, watercolor, cut-out. 2010, 2017.

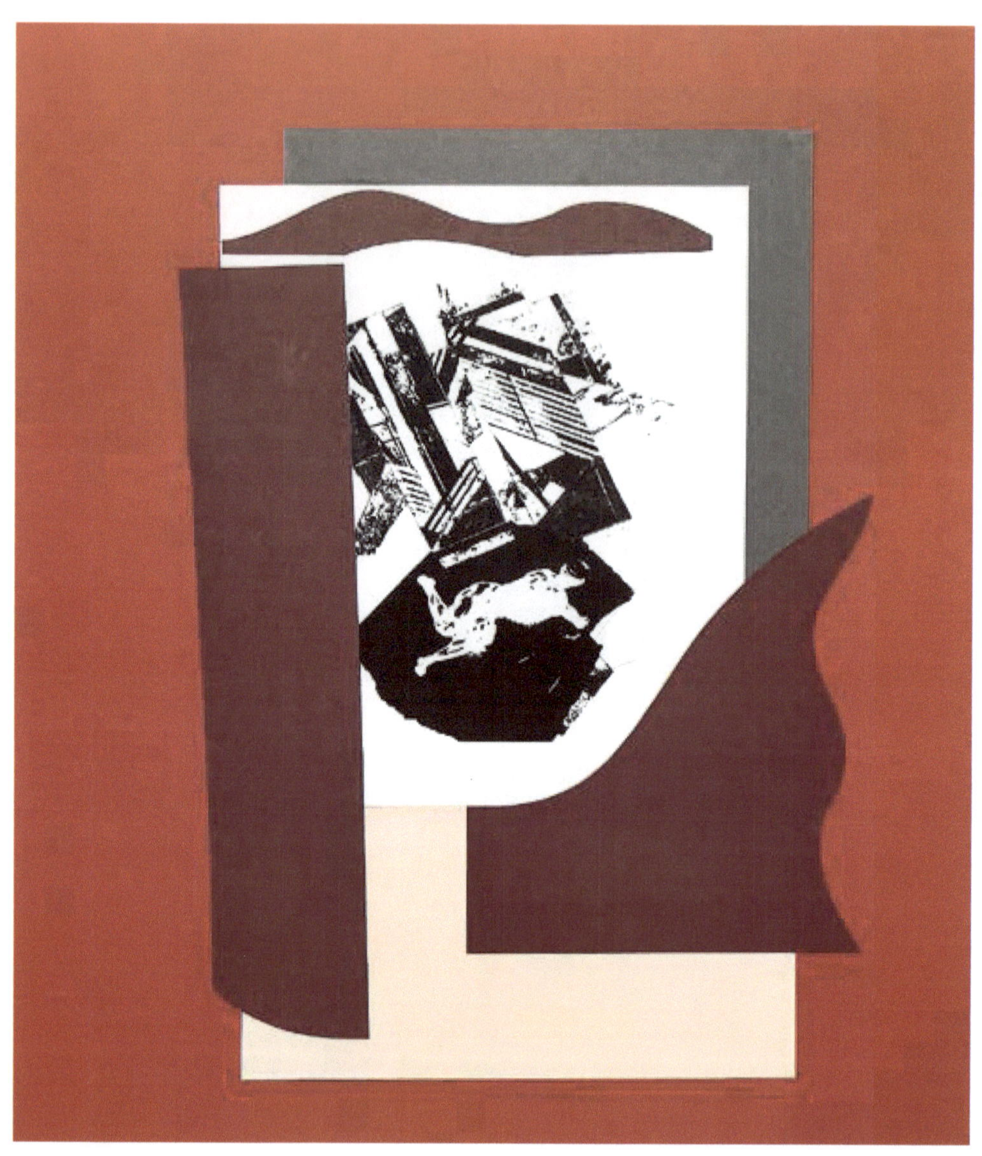

Migraine noir. Ink, cut-out, Renaissance reference. 2015.

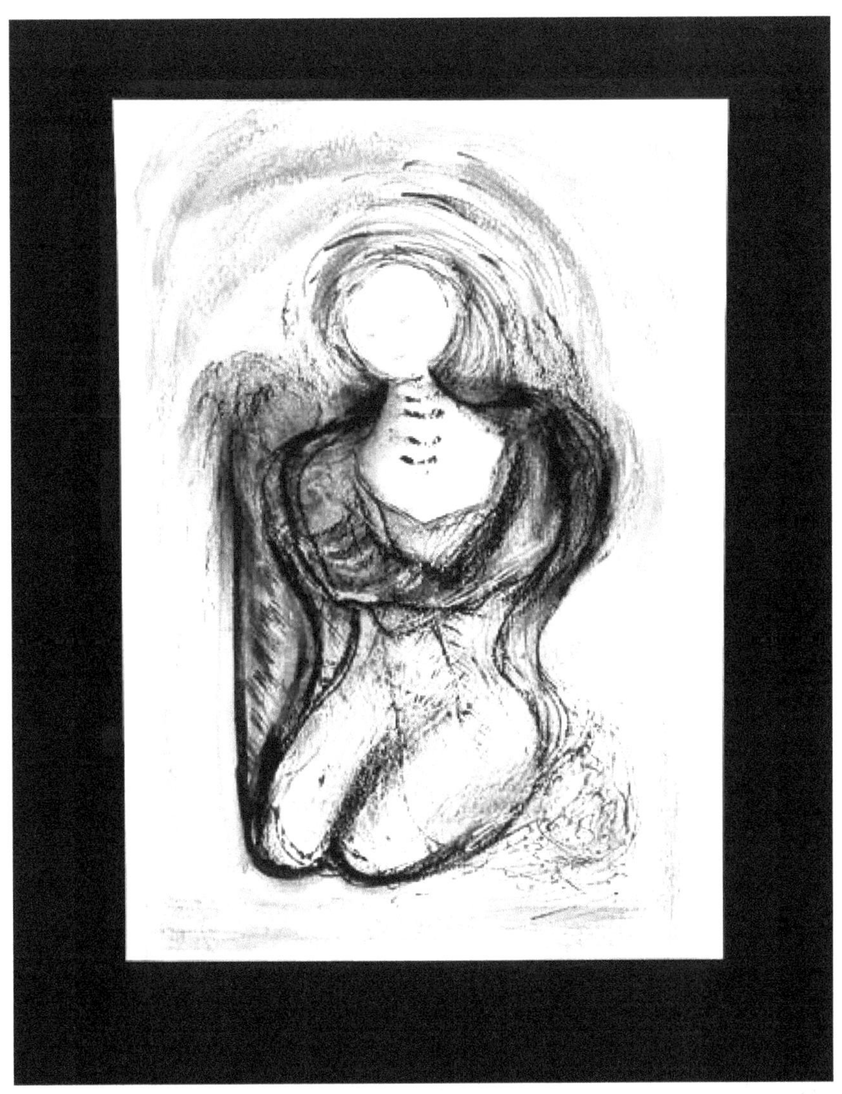

Introspection-DGR-3. Pen and brush ink, acrylic, and graphite. 2022.

“Given the sinister events in its memory,” writes Celan, the language of German poetry has to become “more sober, more factual … ‘grayer.’” This greater factuality checks a core impulse of the lyrical tradition—in German the common word for poetry is Lyrik—and its relation to the lyre, to music: “it is … a language which wants to locate even its ‘musicality’ in such a way that it has nothing in common with the ‘euphony’ which more or less blithely continued to sound alongside the greatest horrors.” The direct effect of giving up this “euphony” is to increase the accuracy of the language: “it does not transfigure or render ‘poetical’; it names, it posits, it tries to measure the area of the given and the possible.”

From the introduction to Paul Celan’s *Breathturn into Timestead: The Collected Later Poetry*, translated by Pierre Joris.

Paul Celan. Edge Recount

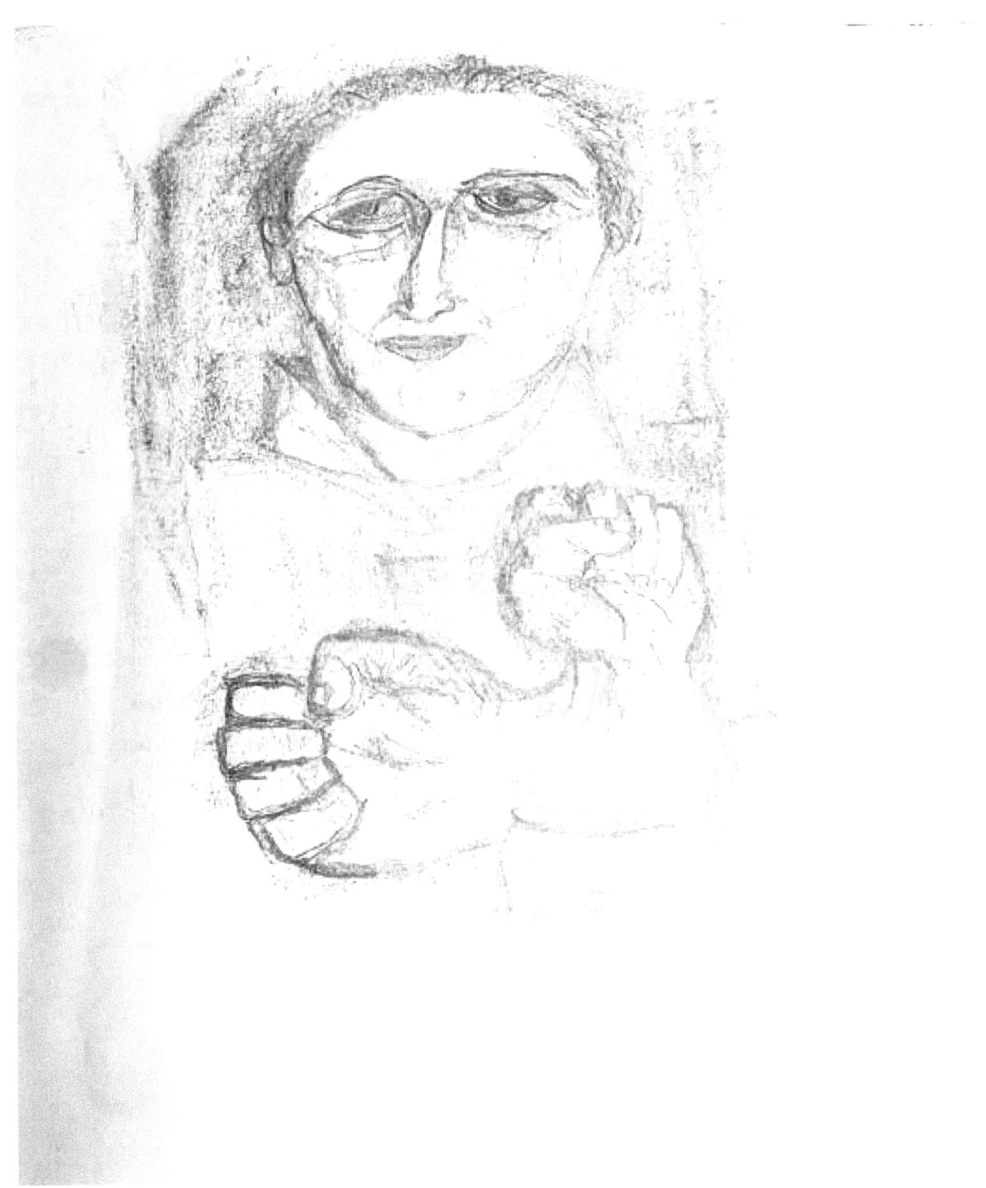

"His arms end in hands he keeps clenched." Graphite. 2024.

"His arms end in hands he keeps clenched"

Engle's Used Books, Berkeley, I picked up Jerome Rothenberg's chapbook of translations, *New Young German Poets*, and read Ingeborg Bachmann's "The Time Allotted," with its first line, "Worse days are coming." The common language toss-off and gloom incurred the acute feeling, a coarsening of dread millions experienced since the drop drill 1950s Cold War era, Leftist witch hunt, Union exterminating, CIA Latin America infiltration, **COINTELPRO** FBI Black Power assassinations and takedown, to the destruction of the Vietnam War, and the Kissinger-Nixon "madman theory" bombings of Laos and Cambodia. Even though, as Bachmann states in another poem, "The time allotted for disavowals/ Comes due..." in the ethical library produced with an awareness before or since Auschwitz (or Vietnam-Cambodia), her ethical alert remains internationally ignored. The indifference of international Command.

Her poems, fused with the sensibility of a teenager living through war, the post-war fire-bombed ruins of Germany, and the exposure of the concentration camps, reveal the reality of laying bare "the secret of sickness" Bachmann refers to in another poem, "Psalm." The phrase contains no heroics. It is a disclosure, lived with. The laying bare, through literature, art, and cultural criticism, has proved to be a continued denuding of uncontrollable inhumane maladies inherent throughout the species. In her novel, *Malina*, the narrator and the eponymous character discuss "War and Peace" as a topic:

> Me: It's called that because one follows the other, isn't that the way it is?
> Malina: It isn't war and peace.
> Me: What is it then?
> Malina: War.
> Me: How am I ever supposed to find peace.
> I want peace.
> Malina: It's war. All you have is this little intermission, nothing more.

There's an imponderable coming to terms with the Holocaust and the developed consciousness of violence of World War Two, directing the tone of almost all the poems in *New Young German Poets*. Specifically, Paul Celan's "A Death Fugue" ("Todesfuge"), was a poem I needed in a personal racial sense. I was aware of the Holocaust since I was eight, 1957. Our parents sat me and my older brother in front of the television to watch Nazi Concentration Camps documentary footage of "that which happened." The impression and stunned questions. Infliction through images. Identification inflicted. Close to that time, my father, agitated and abrupt, recounted what happened to his fourteen-year-old father. Who never once spoke of it. Self-evacuated from his family after a Cossack pogrom. He had walked to another village to buy house paint, then buried himself under leaves in the woods after returning. After seeing his village burning. The filled-up synagogue boarded-up. Set on fire. No longer a Jew, he started on foot three-hundred-something miles from the village woods outside Kiev, to Odessa.
My other grandfather made the same journey, escaping conscription into the advanced guard of the Russian Army, World War One. His family that stayed behind in Kiev, later disappeared into Stalin's Gulag concentration camps.

Celan's "A Death Fugue,"

Black milk of morning we drink you at dusktime
we drink you at noontime and dawntime we drink you at night
we drink and drink
we scoop out a grave in the sky

...the images, the fused sentences, extermination aura, and rhythms of the translation, lent me a remorse for that which happened, and for Ukrainian and Russian Jews what had recently happened before. Accomplished designs for relative outcomes. Happened and happened. Descending back to the Rhineland massacres of The First Crusade, 1096.

When reading Jean Daive's poetic prose memoir *Under the Dome, Walks with Paul Celan*, I started making graphite drawings concerned with impressions I experienced regarding Celan's holocaust trauma, his family losses, those of my family, and what the PTSD had worn out of him by the time of his suicide at age forty-nine, in 1970. Daive's style and content has the reader drawn in and focused for a double lens that never intrudes on what he discloses about his personal relationship with Celan, since we realize that he too has suffered from traumatizing events. Though details of incest are alluded to, but not specifically given, we know by the following statements there is a concrete but unarticulated disaster that shaped him, "Being incapable of speaking had long made my life impossible when I met Paul Celan..." "Being incapable of articulating an absence behind absence plunges me into life" (38, 39). Trauma, punishing experience remembered, and intruding on his present consciousness, forced Celan into the strain and focus of what violated him, exterminated others, and created a source of paradoxical absence. It is not the sole subject, but a generally non-sentimentalized quality of the holocaust derived absences he responds to in his later poems.

It is this absence, not emptiness, and the vicissitudes behind his audible emotions and sensations, that Celan's strongest poems arrive at. Murder. Absence not emptiness. In a common detail Daive recollects this tension from Celan's unexpressed-pre-expressed conflict: "his arms end in hands he keeps clenched" (78).

In *Paul Celan, Poet, Survivor, Jew*, John Felstiner recounts that Celan, who admired existentialist philosopher Martin Heidegger, was invited to his Black Forest retreat. When he arrived, he wrote in the guest book some poetic lines concluding, "with a hope for a coming word in the heart," meaning in direct goodwill "a hope" for Heidegger, a supporter of Nazism, to recognize the catastrophe of what happened and, thereby, in some form of humility, to recant, to bond, or at least intimately sympathize with a traumatized survivor of fascist German ideology and violence. It did not come about. Neither was the hoped-for apology delayed. It was non-existent. The malady itself, Bachmann's the sickness laid bare, the "secret of sickness" maintains malignant forms. Intricately related to global systems of economic elitism, militarized hierarchy, racial and cultural discrimination, it exists in the violent leadership, and those that adhere to it, in

Israel and the Arab countries, in the United States, in Europe, in Russia, in China, in Latin America, etc. The hate-grudge and the dominance entitlement grudge are not an enigma. Psychologically, cultural treatment remains fatuous. It is an apparently obliterated intent. For people that have suffered from the malignancy, there are the lingering and violent erosive facts of traumatic dissolution. The arms that end in hands Paul Celan keeps clenched, is an objective metaphor. A reactive tribute.

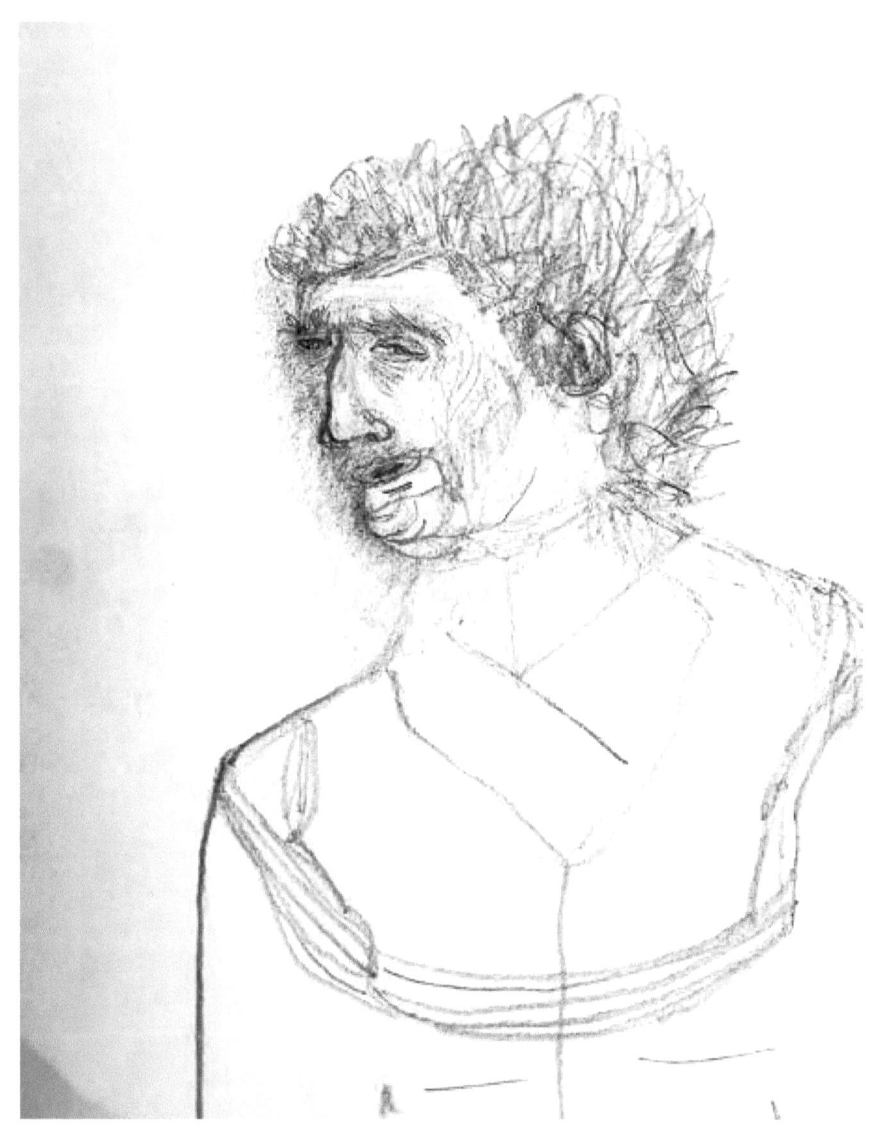

Paul Celan. Mourner 1. Graphite. 2024.

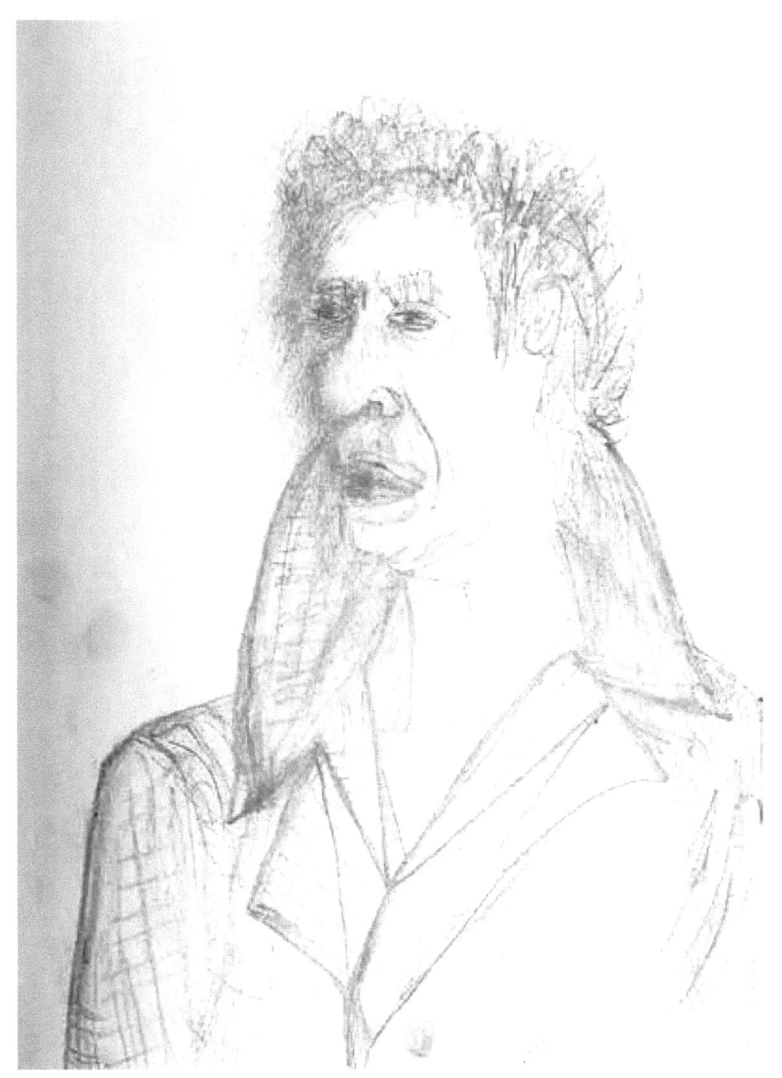

Paul Celan. Mourner 2. Graphite. 2024.

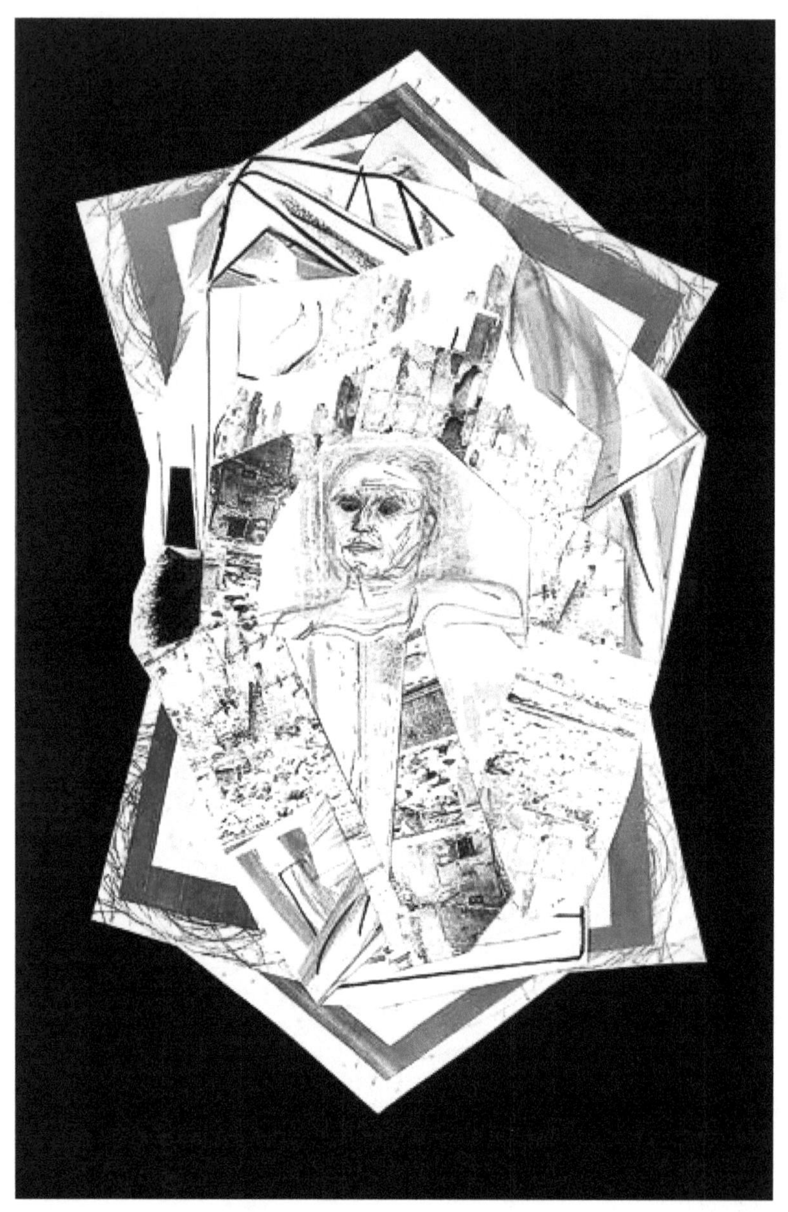

Paul Celan. Mourner 3. Ink, acrylic, photograph, cut-out. 2024.

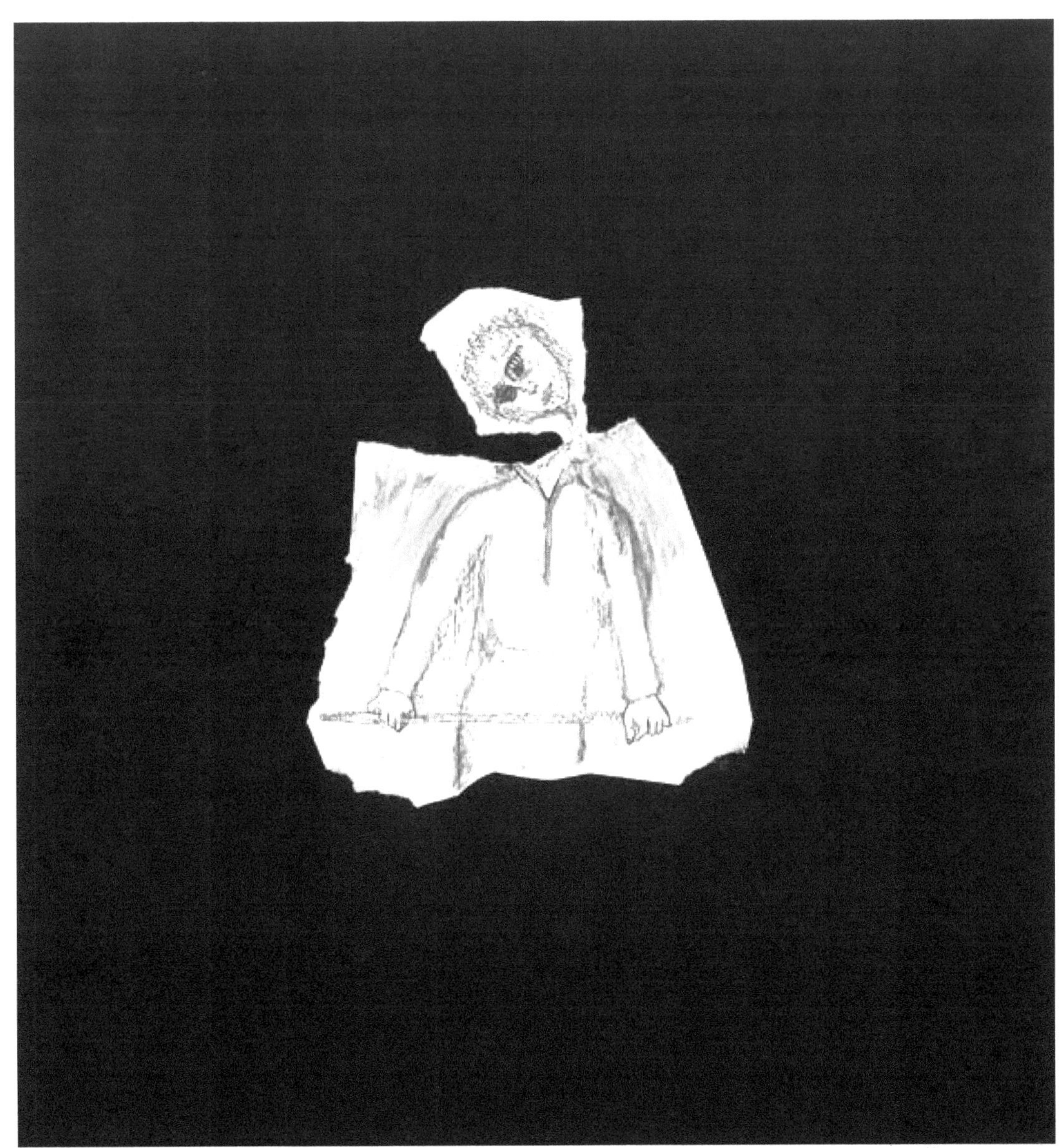

Paul Celan. Mourner 4. Graphite. 2024.

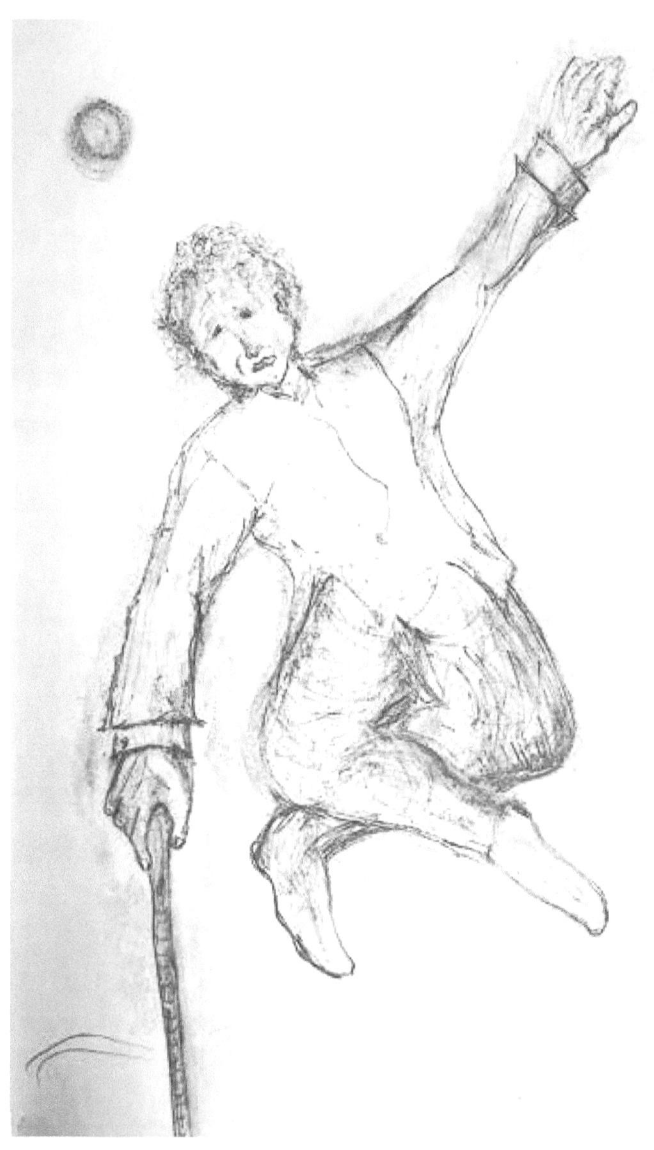

Leo Celan. DeathTango. Walking stick. Graphite. 2024. Celan's father, murdered in an internment camp in Romania.

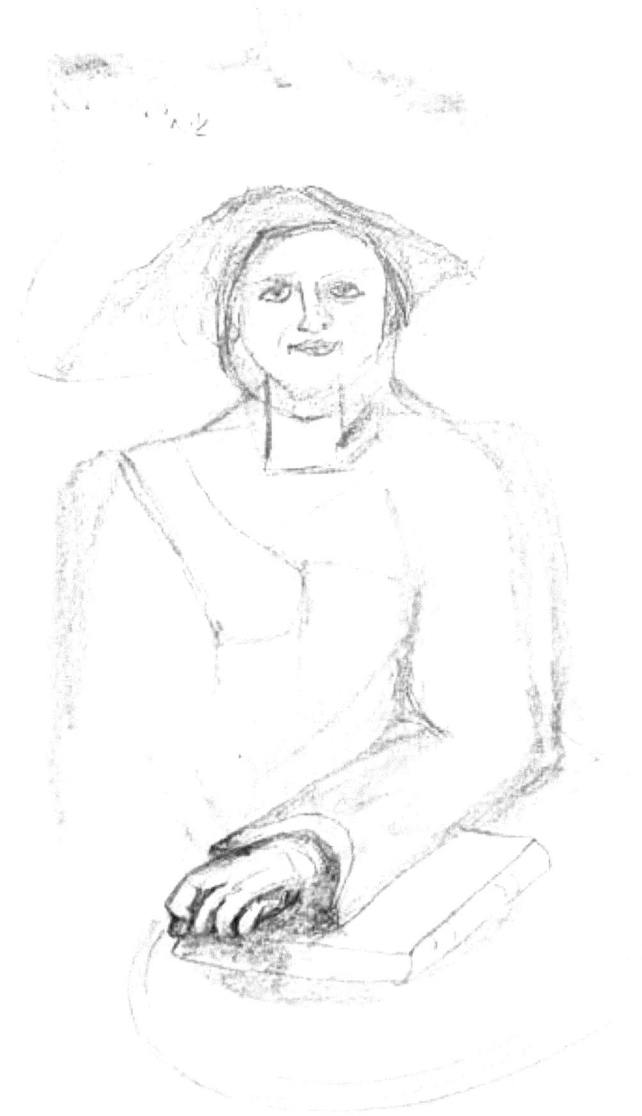

Fritzi Celan. Heavier dog. Graphite. 2024. “Fritzi,” Celan’s mother, murdered with her husband in an internment camp in Romania.

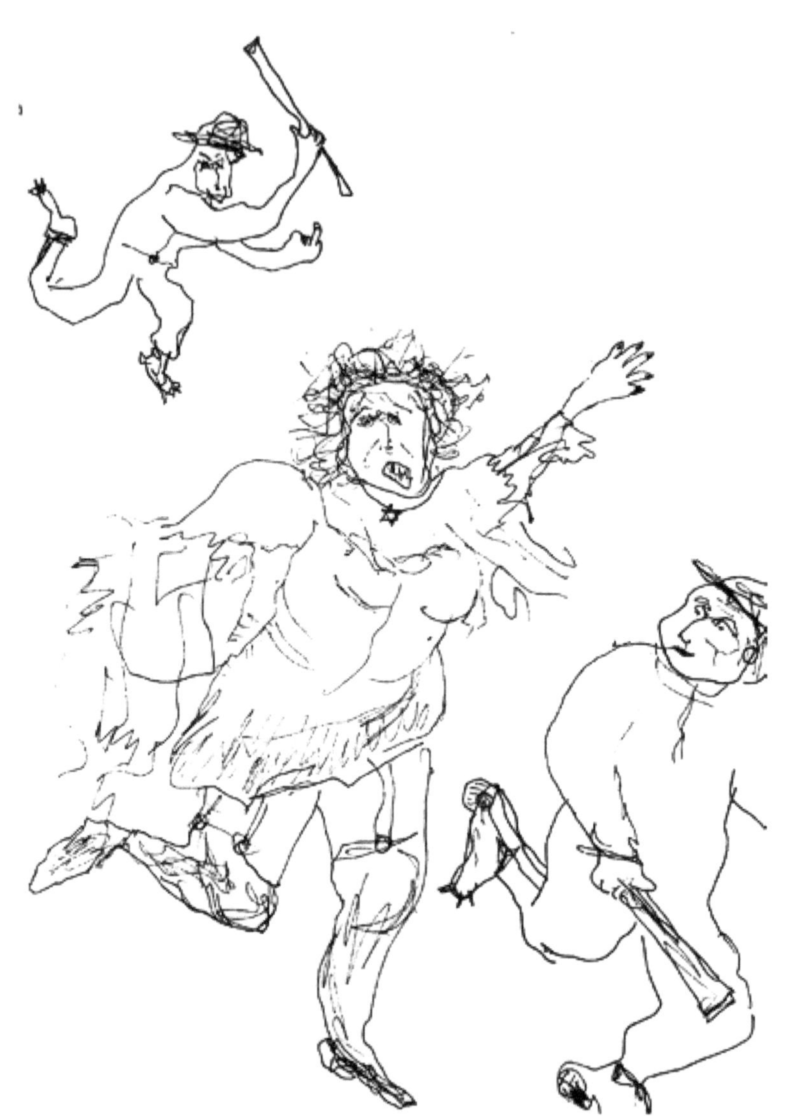

Pogrom escapee. Ink pen. 2018.

Jewdog

I turn the page with my tongue to study an enlargement of the frog
and two small, armored dogs—I study the Fury with a jawbone of nails pressing behind them.
My nose moistens over the pet devil guarding a nun.
I turn the page to study the painted layers of a knight's armor
and the mast of a boat with a cargo of hands.
I'm licking the paint for the last time
looking at Hieronymus Bosch for the last time
looking at Saint Anthony and the virgin blood
in the human-sized frog's cup for the last time.
I lick the shrubs where the dogs came through,
erasing them,
erasing the painted table and the painted path,
erasing the cleaver and the bowls prepared
for the dog's meat.
I'm chewing on Alain Resnais's celluloid.
The plumber who puts in the gas-line not a waterline
to the showers goes down in the acids
of my saliva, cursing Jews.
The celluloid cracks around my eyelids.
I lick off the smoldering edges,
I lick the paint off an idiot's head,
I lick the paint of the pet devil for the last time,
I erase the painted egg it produced,
I lick the closed door of the tiled room and the leather sweatband
of a helmet a guard left against the door jamb.
I lick the German conductor's fingers,
they smell of dumplings and vaginal juice
I lick the threshold of the door where the music carries you away.
But they went off already, the procession of Jews.
The armored dogs too are going, the get-up they're in won't matter.
I'm looking at the winged executive for the last time.

I run at the legs of a girl who is the color of ripened limes
I do it so she'll get out of here if she doesn't know.
I watch him land on the table where she sleeps.
I watch him and the guards preparing
the lime-colored one for the last time.
He's taking her bladder to transplant for his pet Rottweiler,
he's taking her hair for the heads of his upholstered dolls.
His legs reach across the room.
I watch him jar the bladder in the preserving solution.
I watch him fold the hair down for the last time.
Looking into her open skin he says,
"I do not have roses, I do not need roses, but you
you are a lime wrapped in a rose,
you must pay for your rose, have you forgotten?"
Nothing but hair rolled by hand into separate stacks.
Nothing but French ants, German ants, Croatian
and Ukrainian ants carrying their packages of hair away.
Nothing but papers for transport, helmet liner contracts,
little death-carts of hair, nothing but weaponry salesmen
departing for the Mideast.
I'm licking her feet, I'm washing the lime-colored one's feet
staring down at the linoleum of Portland, sweating into the booth,
eating in there, writing and pausing. Nothing but a Jew's dream.

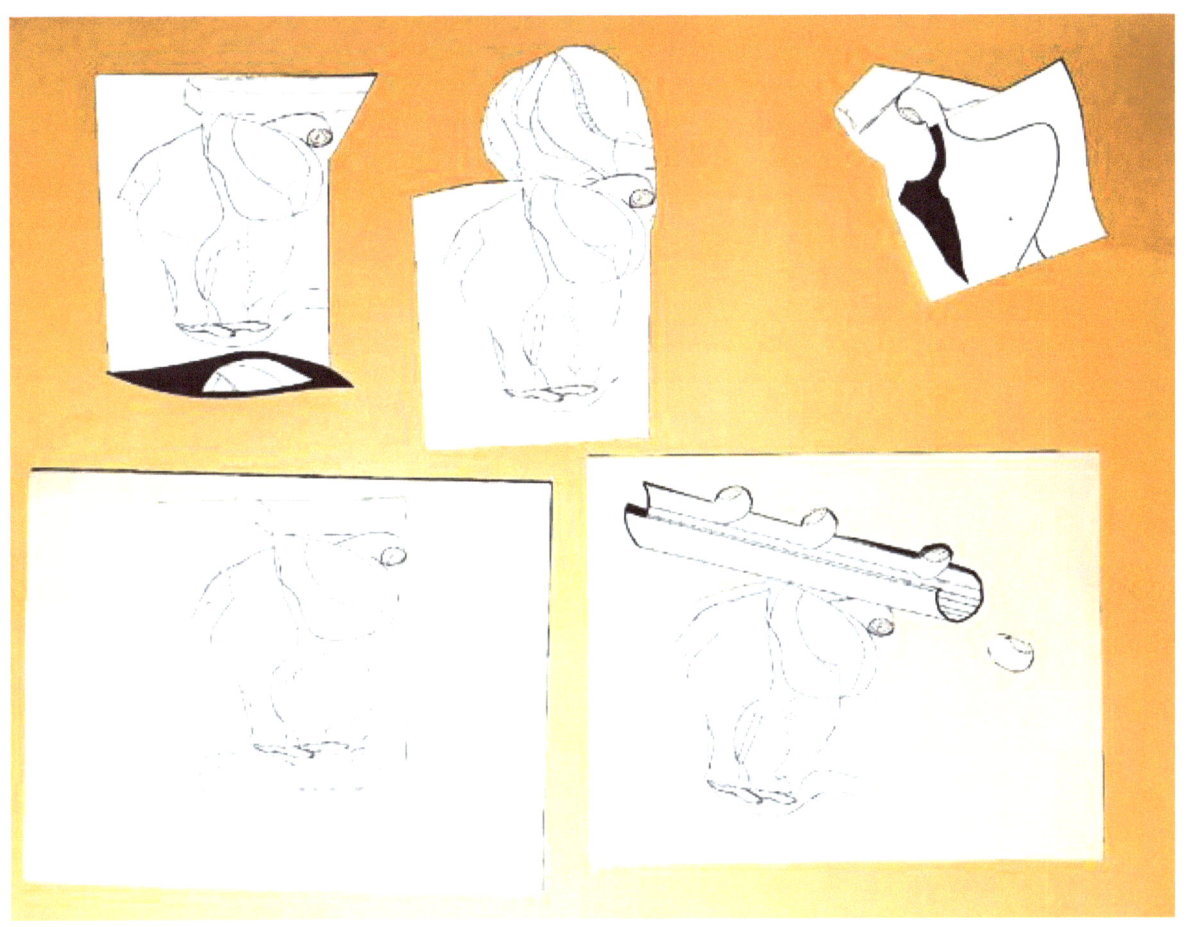

Removing rubble, relocation camp. Ink. 2023.

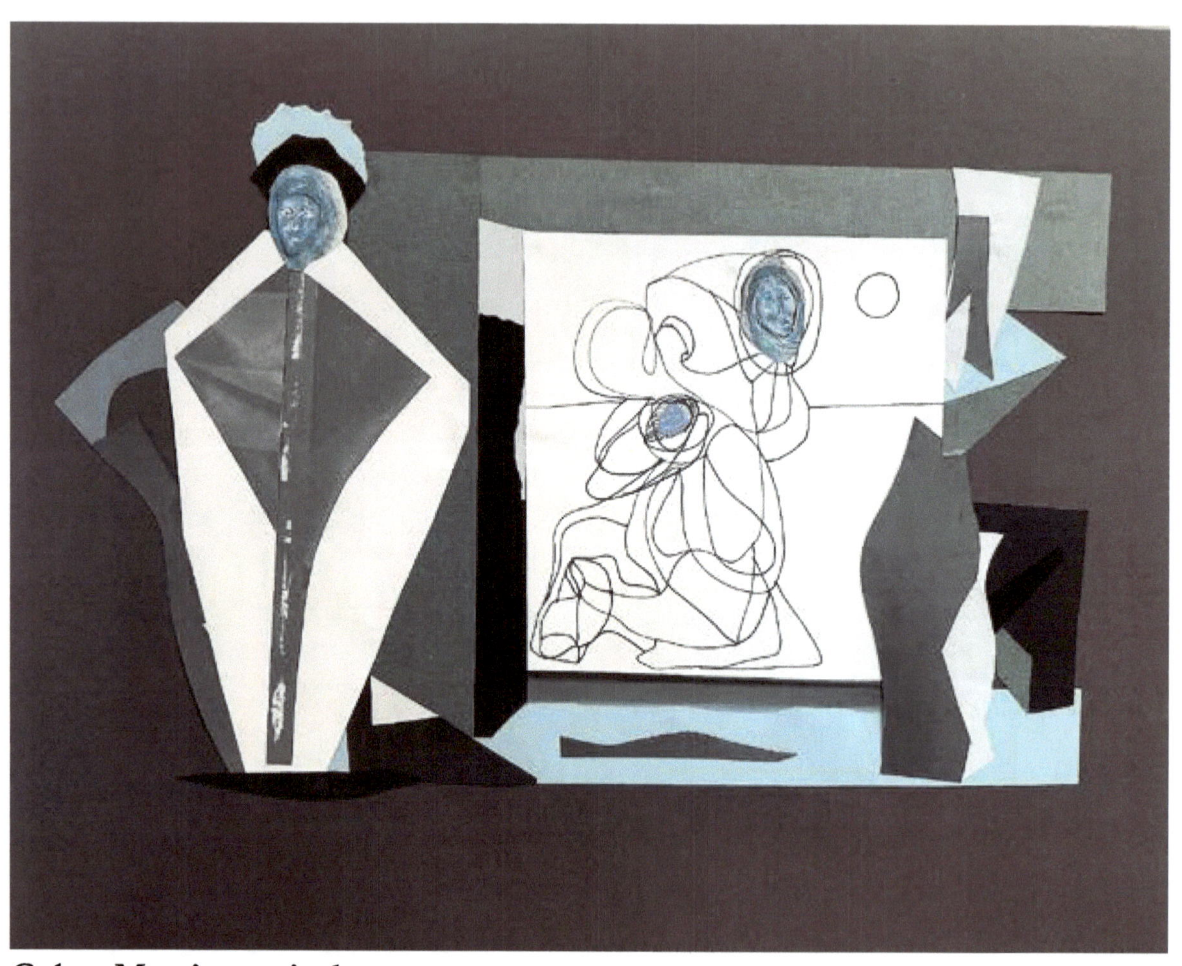

Gabor Mate's survival. Watercolor, acrylic ink, collage, cut-out. 2020.

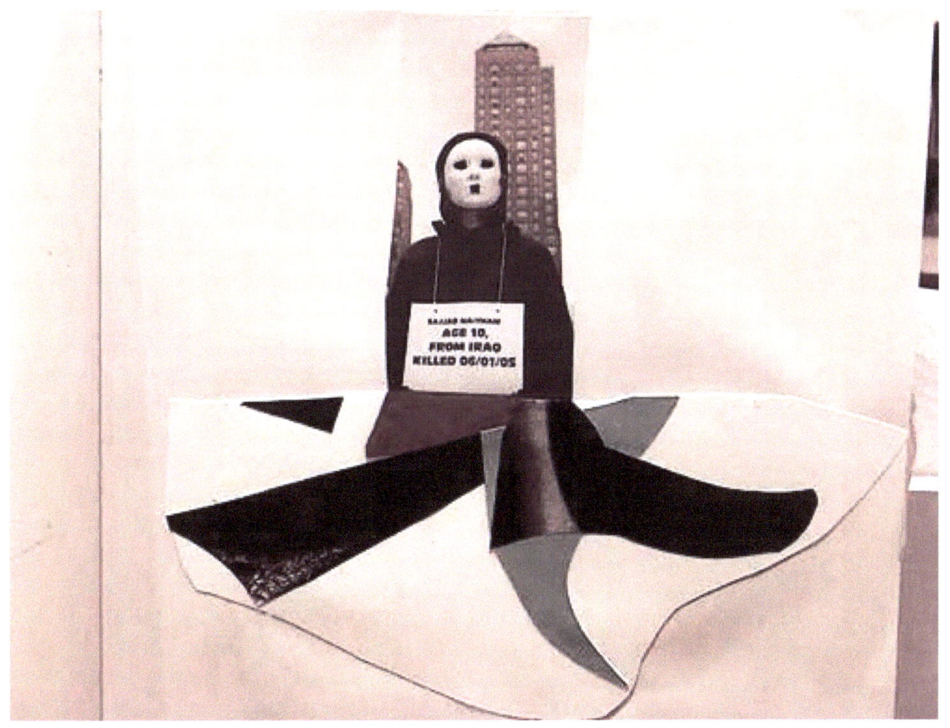

Title in the image. Photomontage and cut-outs. 2003, 2014.

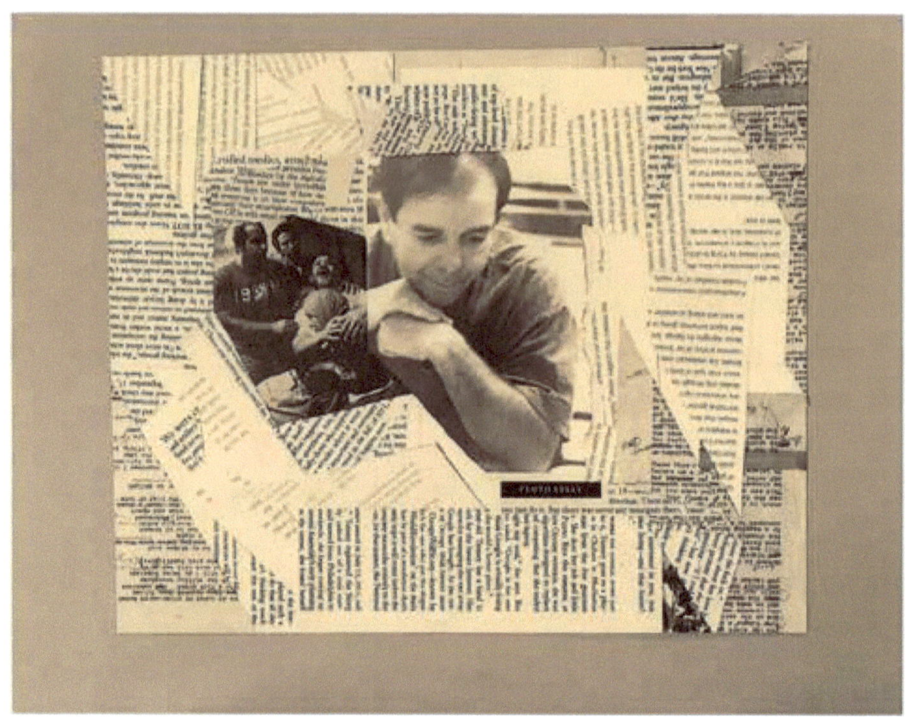

Photo essay documents. Text and photomontage. 2010. Photo of Gary Robbins by LD Janakos.

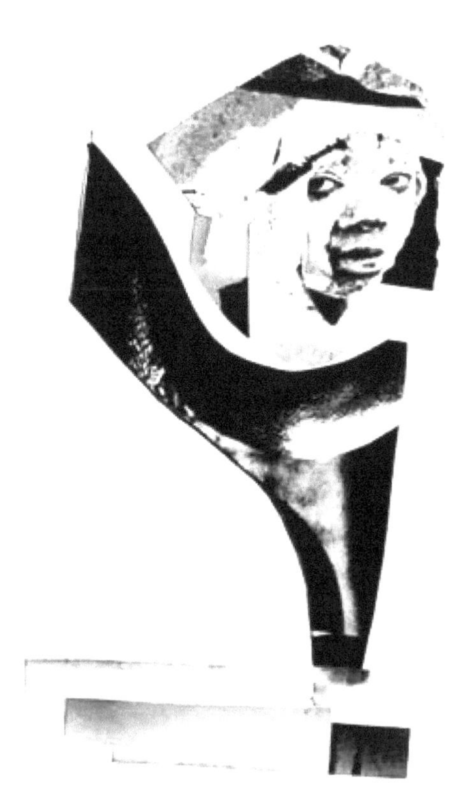

Black nephew archetype. Ink, photomontage, cut outs. 2017.

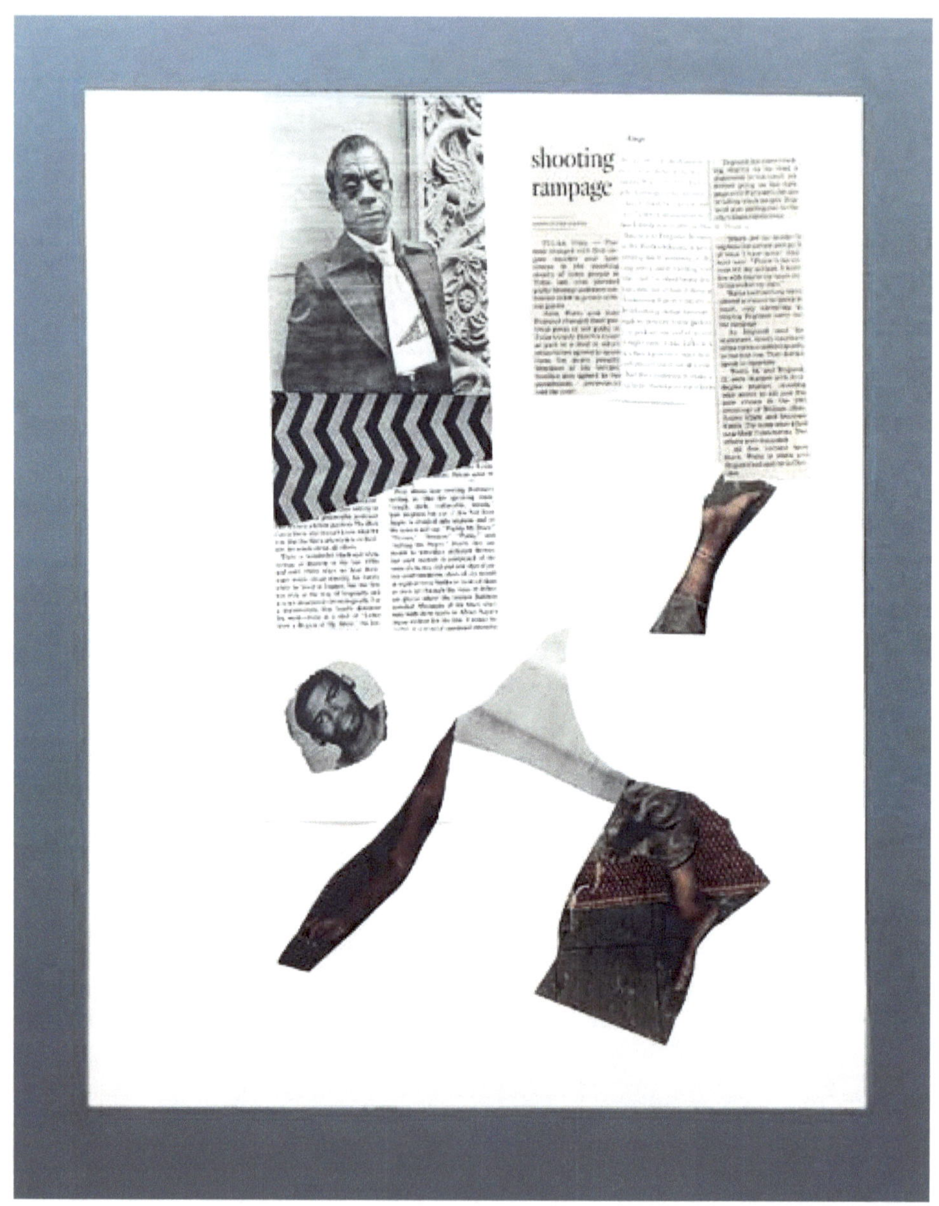

James Baldwin observes. Text, cut-out, and photomontage. 2012.

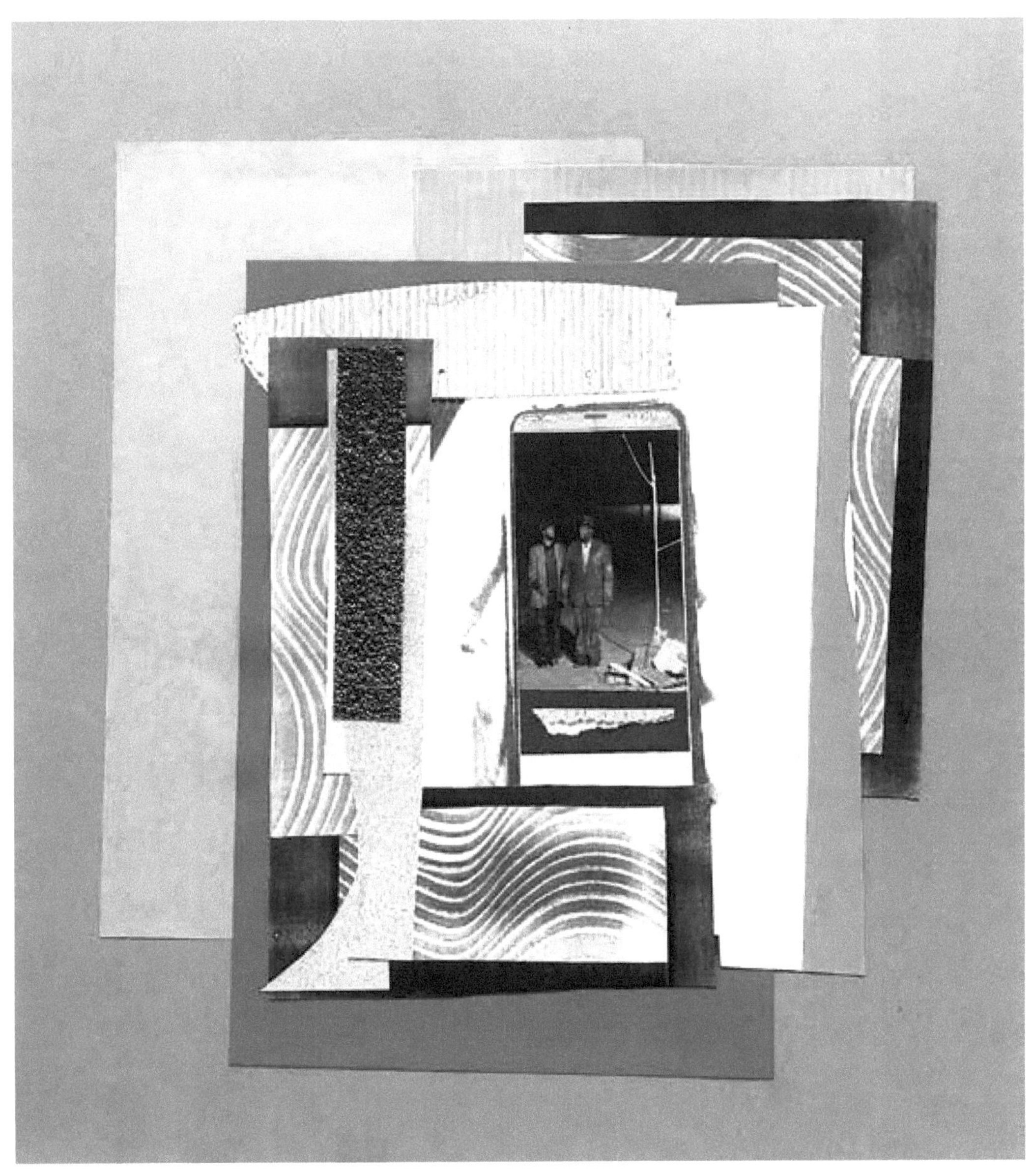

Waiting for Godot Mutherfucker. Ink, cut-out, and photomontage. 2014.

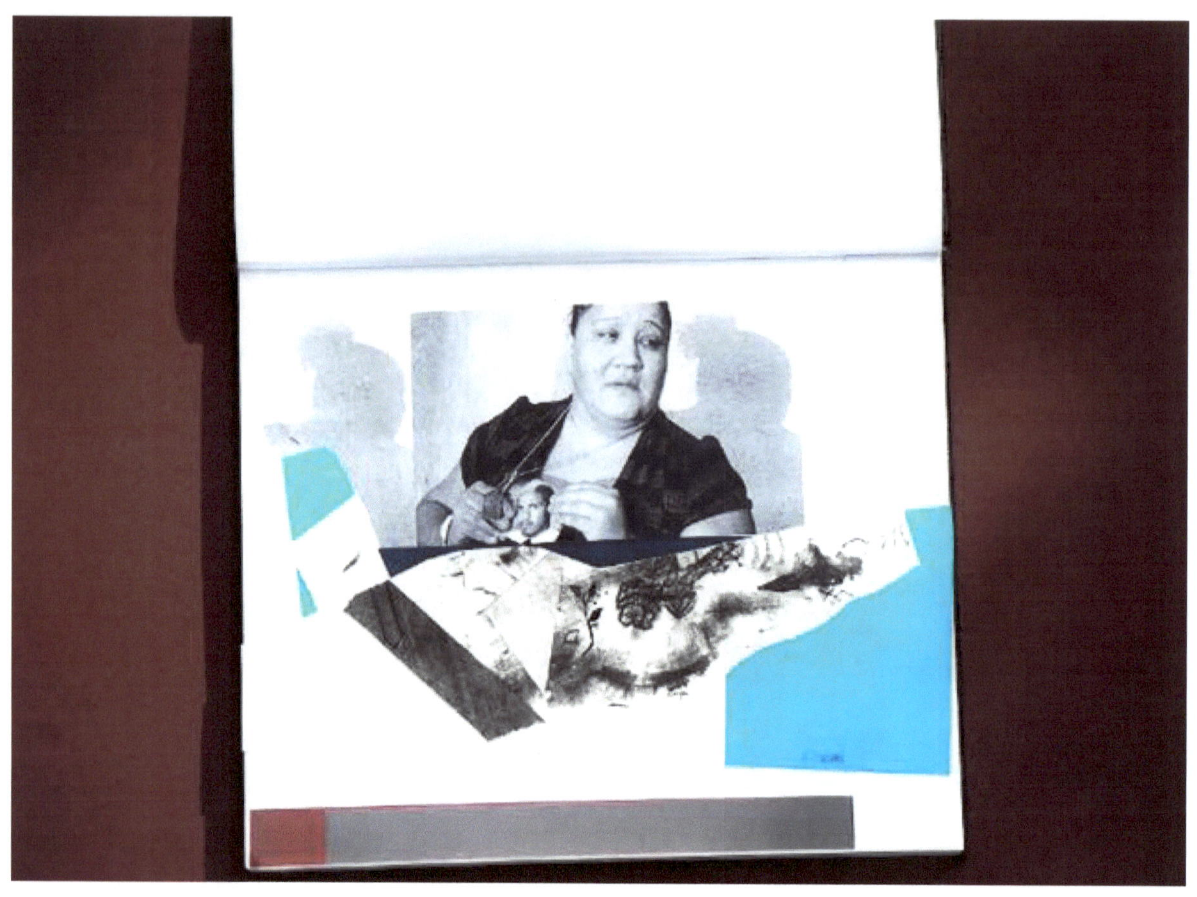

U.S. mother disappeared Veteran son. Photomontage, ink, cut-outs. 2010.

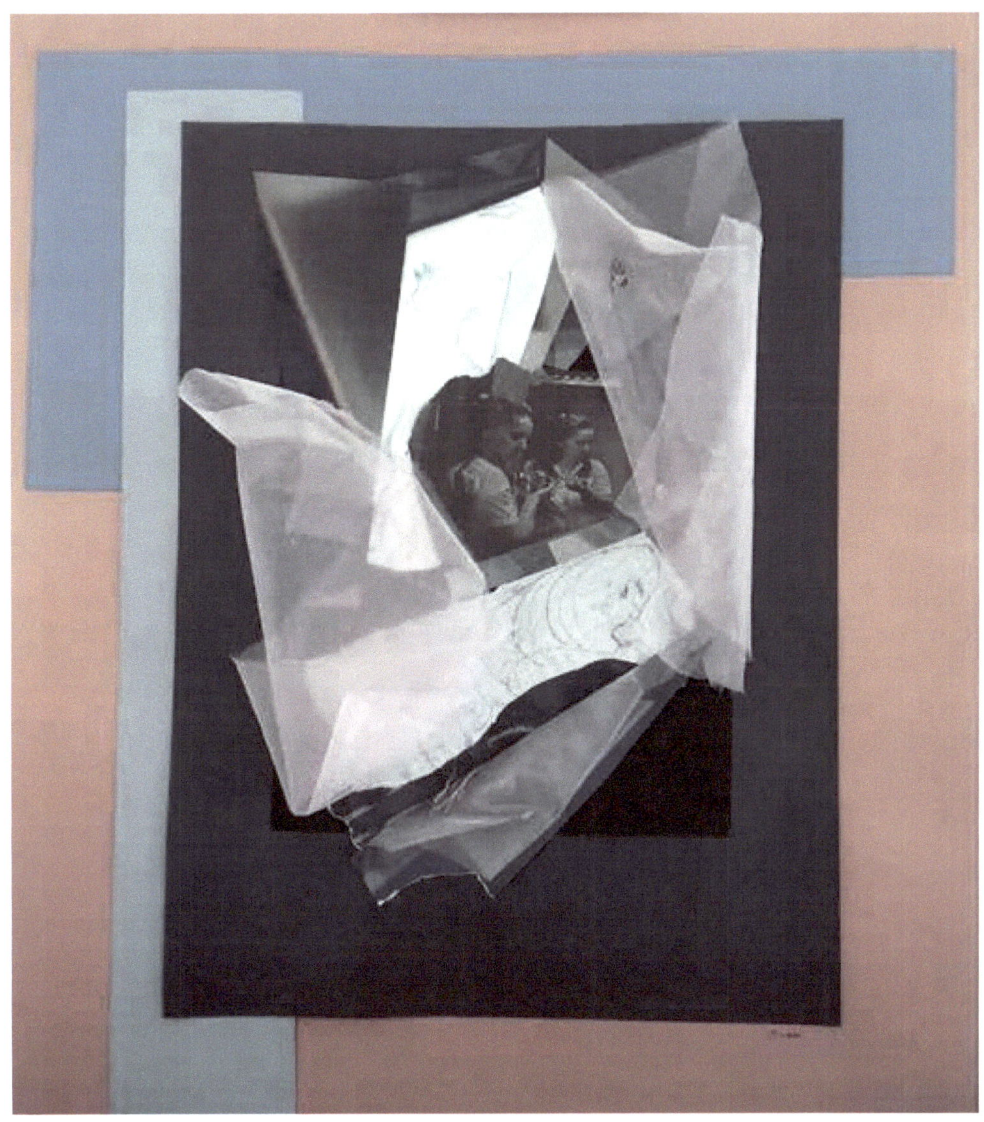

Mother of permanently disabled Vet. Watercolor, assembled cloths, photomontage, cut-outs, ink. 1979, 1983, 2012.

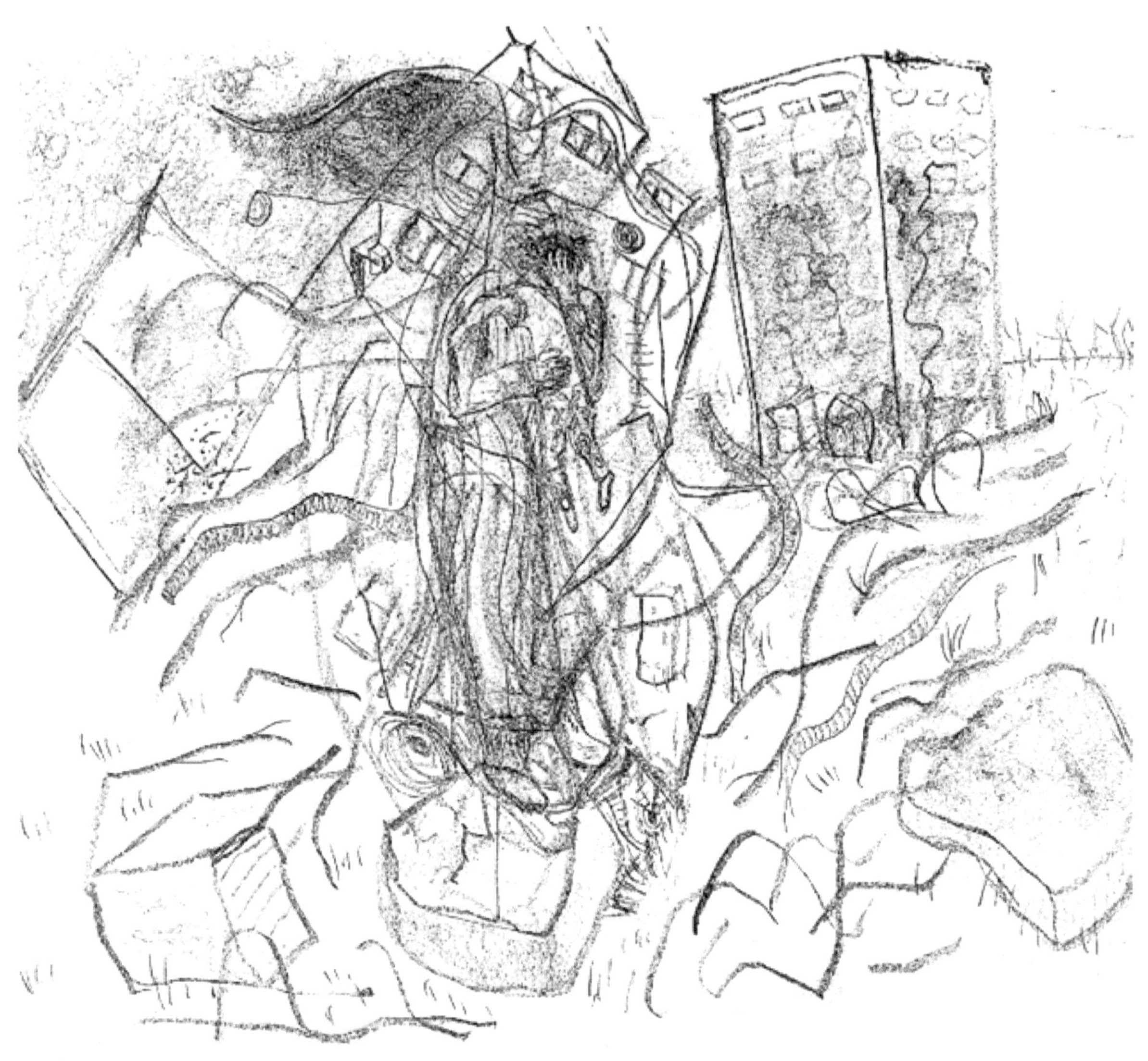

Gaza, Palestinians. Multiple dates. Ink.

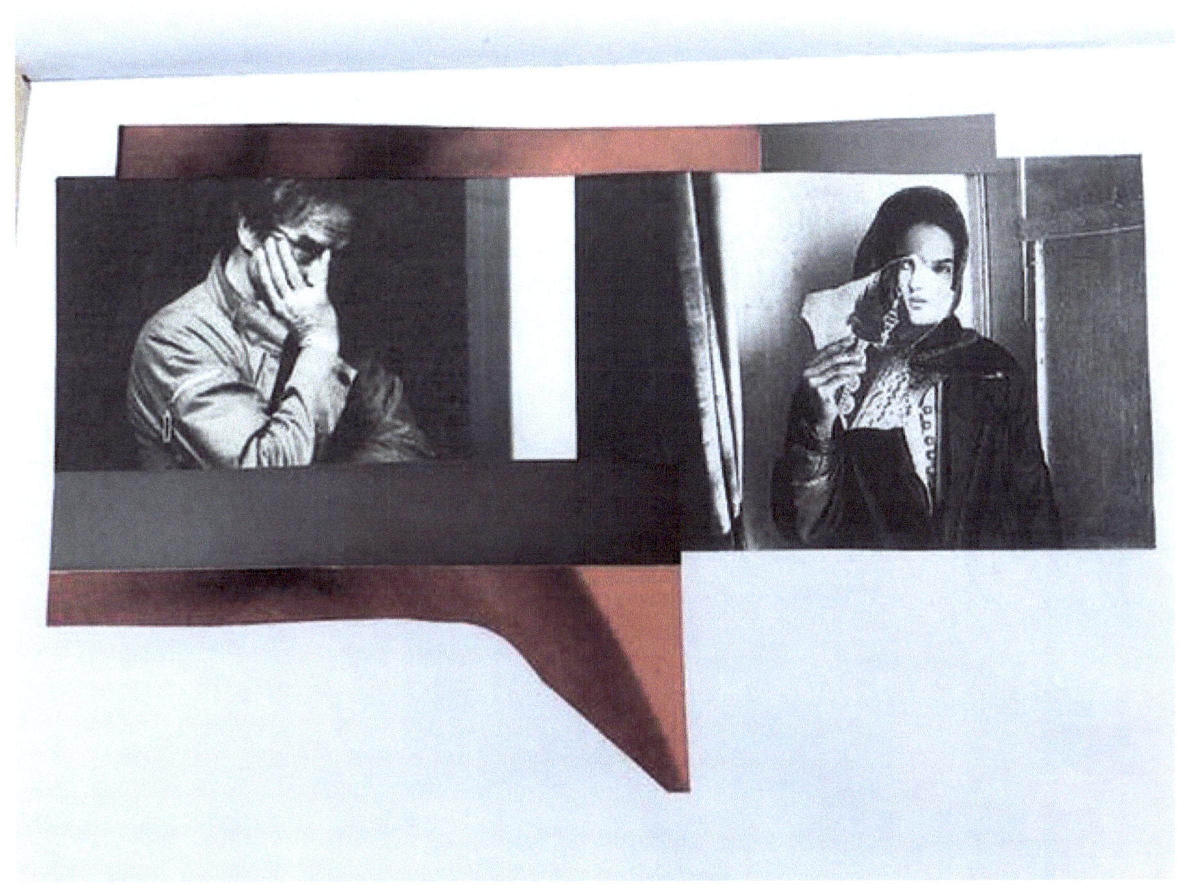

John Cassavetes observes. Photomontage and cutouts. 2015.

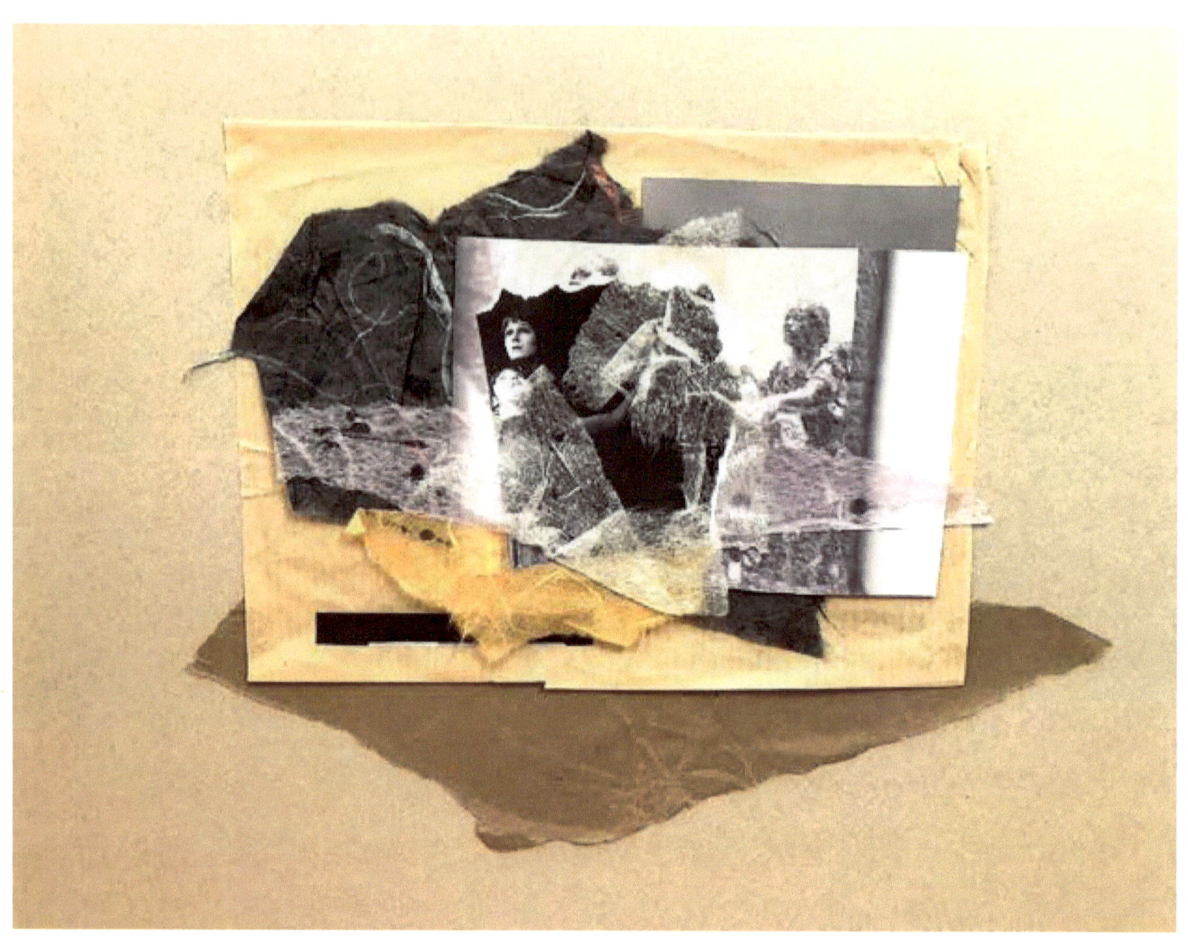

White and Black Antigone. Cloth, cut-outs, photomontage. 2014.

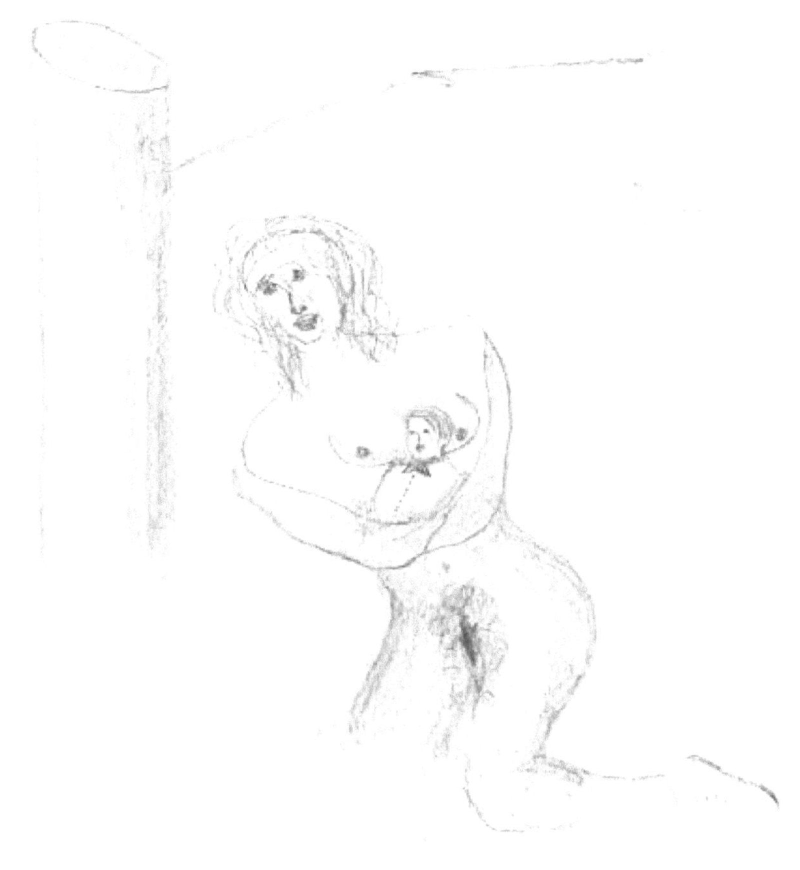

Baby Hitler with wet nurse. Graphite. 2024.

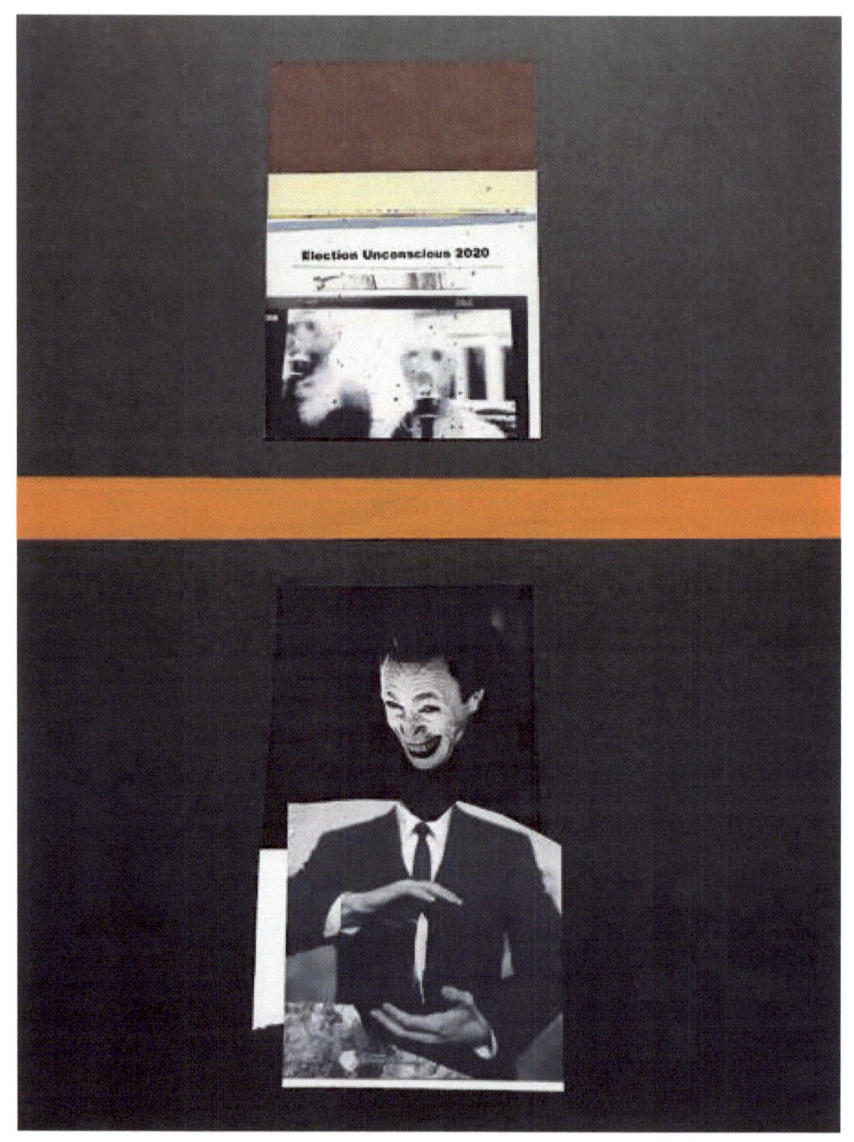

Elections in my time. Photomontage, cut outs. 2019.

Erotic Feelings One

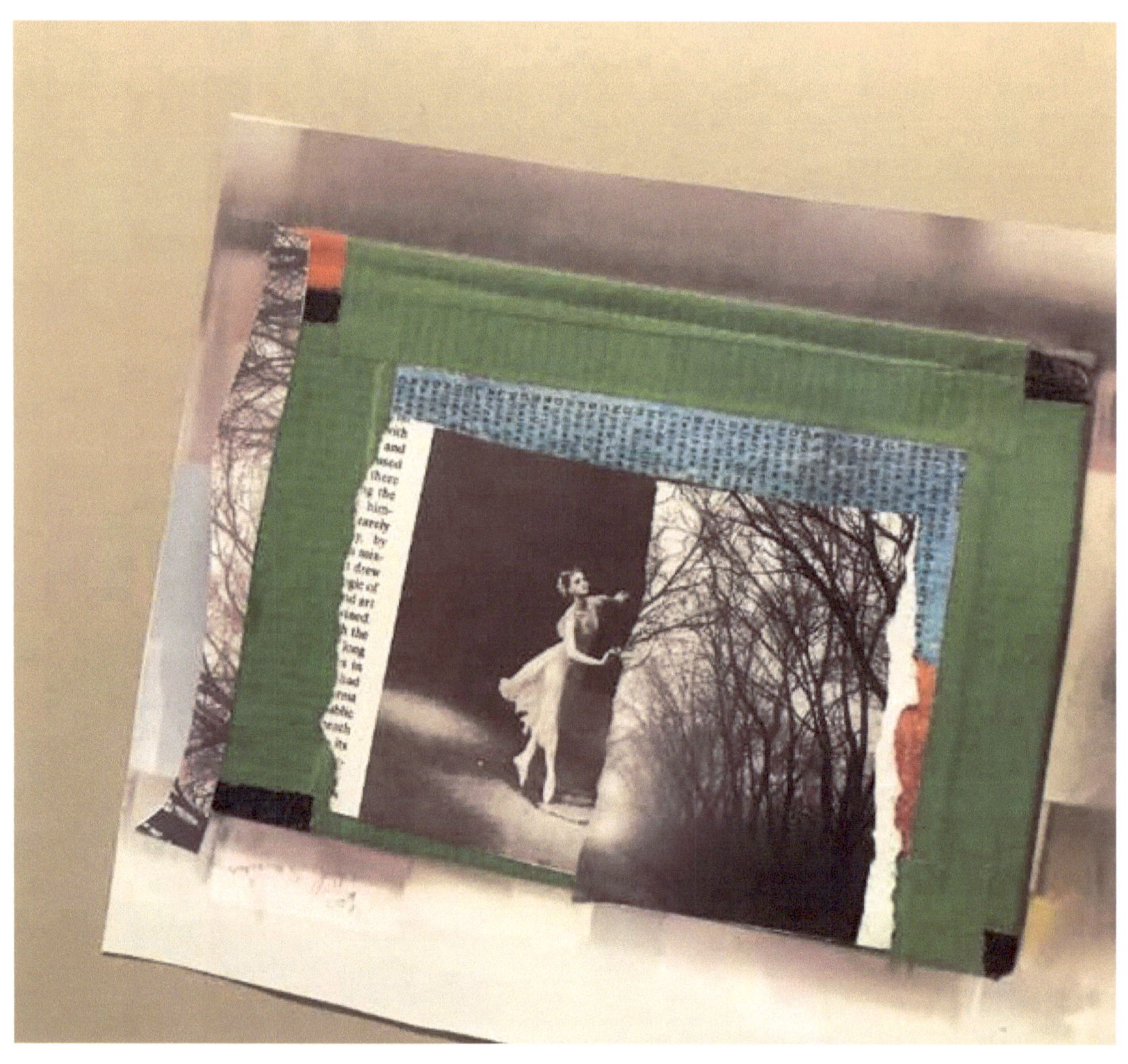

Boundary in the title 1. Photomontage, ink, cut-outs, assembled materials. 2011.

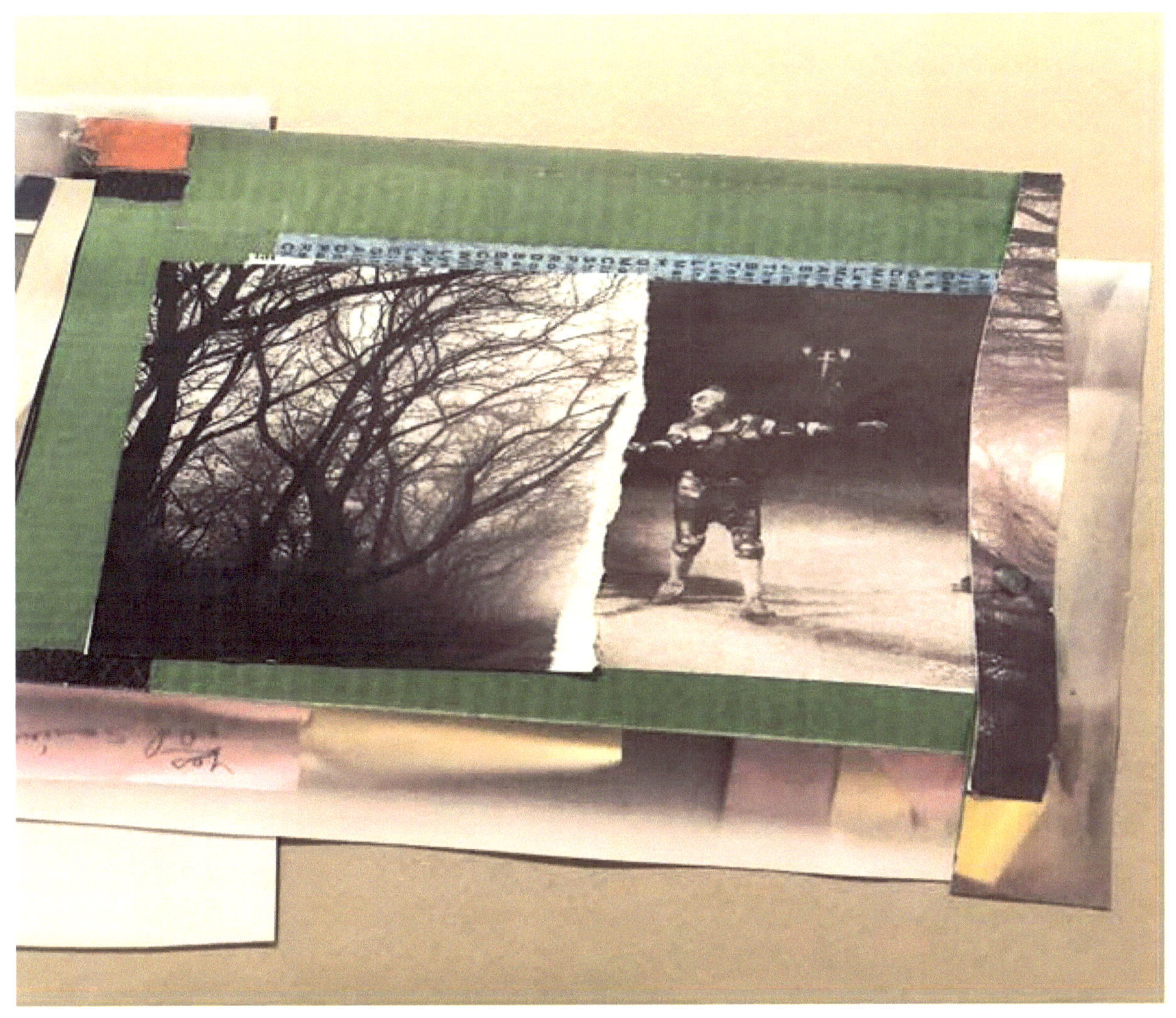

Boundary in the title 2. Photomontage, ink, cut-outs, assembled materials. 2011.

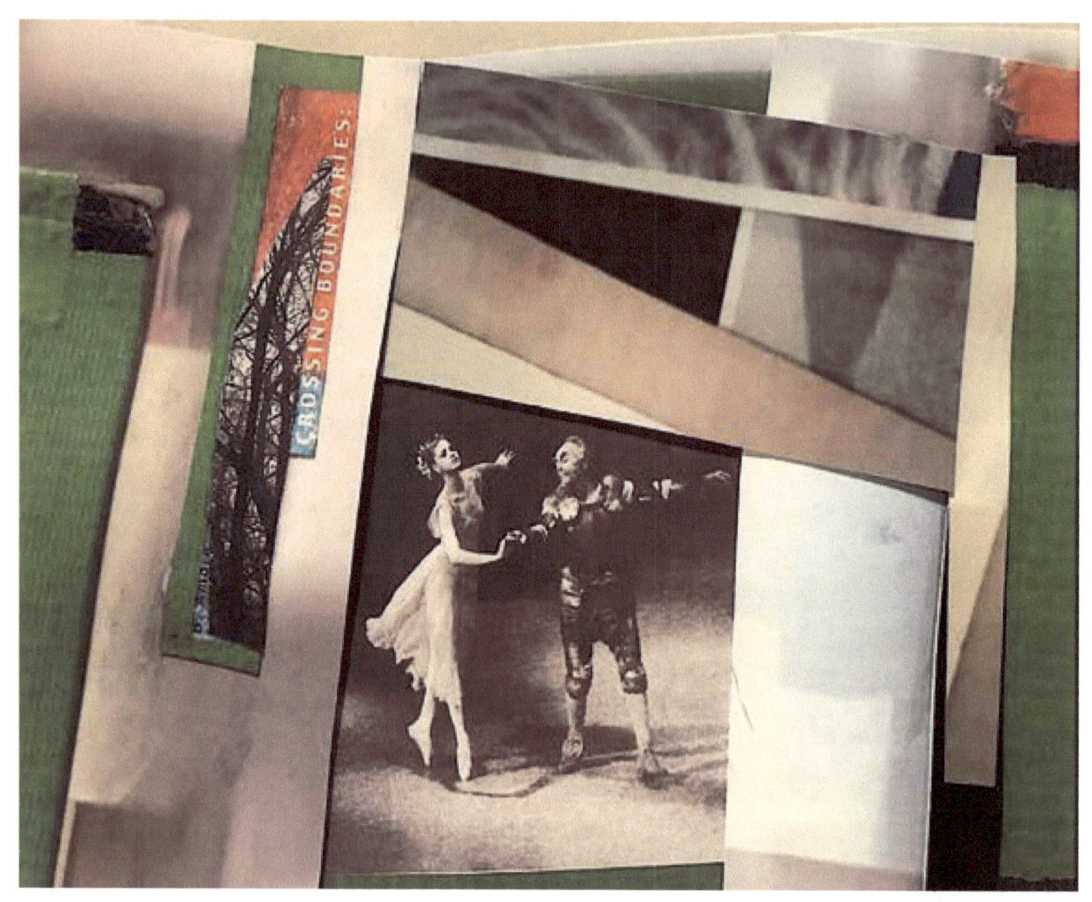

Boundary in the title 3. Photomontage, ink, cut-outs, assembled materials. 2011.

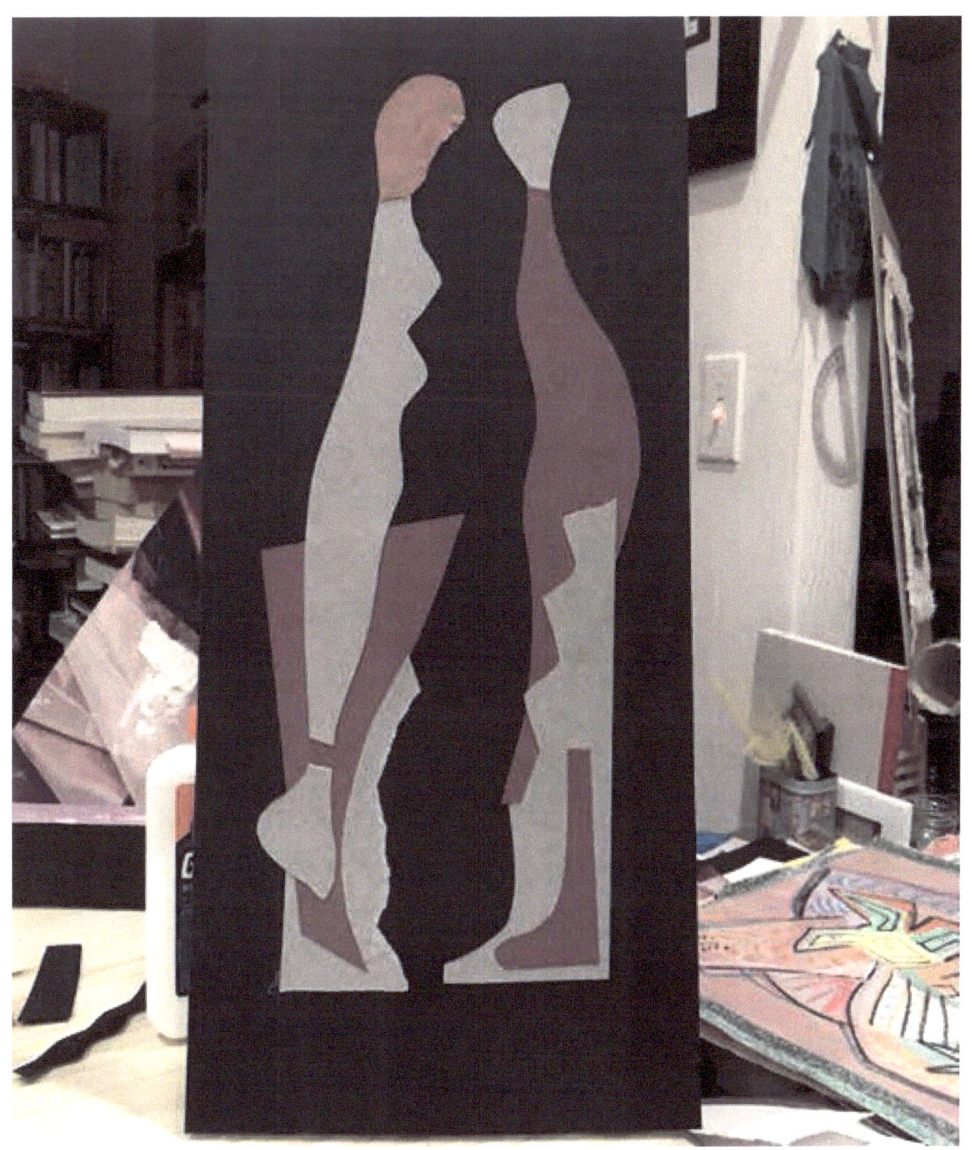

Night kiss, studio build-up. Cut-outs. 2013.

The Sexiest Part

The sexiest part is the way she clipped two-year-old's fingernails with patience.

The sexiest part is the way she read at night to our abandoned three-year-old nephew and when he finally slept she made actual plans either to adopt or abduct him because his young mother was cruel and didn't care that she was.

The sexiest part—that she still took her step-niece and stepdaughter for school notebooks and pencils, took them to the Natural History Museum and to the park with the struggling tire-swing and to see the Mermaid movie and all that, although almost everyone in the family
tried to divide us for five years.

Our life together is my fetish, my connection, my lucky fit. The sexiest part is the unpredictable switch in her stance which I relate to a mare in heat I saw once when they led a stallion around the other side of a corral until later.

The sexiest part is that she is not "sexy" she is mild in a way that protects the exotic aura about her.

The sexiest part is when my face washes out and her face washes over it, and we rest on the side of her hair.

The sexiest part is the powerless magic of not parting but magic, nonetheless.

Iron Heel Series

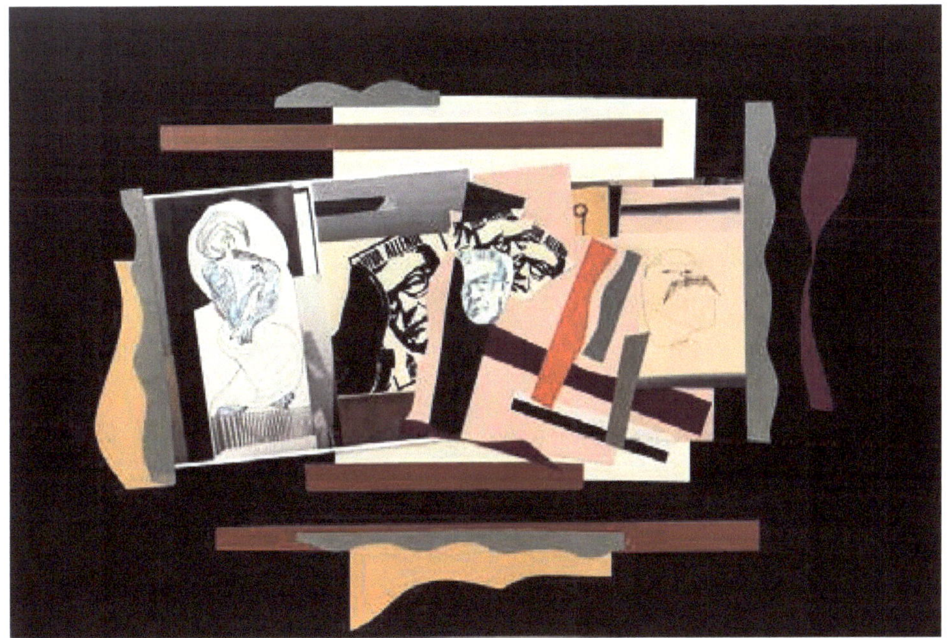

The Iron Heel Sequence 1. Photomontage, ink, and cut-outs. 2016.

The "Iron Heel Sequence" (mixed media photomontage 2016-2019) began with a sighting of the Lawrence Hill & Co. Publishers book cover of Jack London's 1908 revolutionary novel *The Iron Heel* (the artist is anonymous). From a Marxist view of surplus value, exploitation, and alienated labor, it is a lucid and sometimes awkwardly written narrative depicting an earlier violent situation of our class society under the militarist and mercenary powers of the oligarchy maintaining the United States caste system of wage slavery. In a critical discussion over the inevitable violence between the unemployed and the working-class against the oligarchy and the government, Mr. Wickson, a representative force of the oligarchy, forcefully responds to the directly articulate and threatening socialist revolutionary, Ernest Everhard,

> "But not by buzzing will we crush the bear," Mr. Wickson went on coldly and dispassionately. "We hunt the bear. We will not reply to the bear with words. Our reply shall be couched in words of lead. We are the power. Nobody will deny it. By virtue of that power we will remain in power." He suddenly turned upon Ernest. The moment was dramatic. "This then is our answer. We have no words to waste on you. When you reach out your vaunted strong hands for our palaces and purpled ease, we will show you what strength is. In a roar of shell and shrapnel and in the whine of machine-guns will our answer be couched. We will grind you revolutionists down under our iron heel, and we shall walk upon your faces" (63).

As a man with immediate experience of the very poor[1] and as common-sense observer with a Marxist background in perceiving class tensions, Jack London represented class war as the inevitable causation of the deprivations and sufferings of workers enslaved to state, banking, and corporate economic power. The book was published within ten-twelve years of The Espionage Act and The Palmer Raids. These state and ruling class directed laws and events display the methods of oligarchic power when its economic will to control territories, labor unions and resources, demands for waging war, and violently repressing war resisters and unionists, while financially benefitting the oligarchy's institutions and corporations, transparently reveals the class contradictions inherent in the extremely limited economic representation of Liberal Democracy.

"Liberation," what Yevgeny Zamyatin ironically refers to as a "criminal instinct" hasn't yet reached the level of overall neutralization from "the beneficent yoke of the state" that he

[1] Jack London worked, lived with, and wrote about the poor and the working class in his earlier book, *People of the Abyss.*

imagines in his futurist 1920 satire *We*. Though there are revolutionary and oligarchic spies in *The Iron Heel*, there is nothing like Zamyatin's totalitarian understanding of how surveillance in his dystopic "One State" would be implemented through our future (now present) Internet Police, Biometric identification, Surveillance cameras in public places, Geolocation tracking on cellphones/GPS, etc. Zamyatin's prescience is demonstrated in the passage where the engineer-narrator recounts having "recently had to work out the curvature of a new type of street membrane (these membranes, elegantly decorated are now on all the avenues and record street conversations for the Bureau of Guardians)" (53). In Zamyatin's novel, the people of One State all live in glass structures and are literally known to each other through numbered identification. The "glass" image is now a metonym for the near total and panoptic transparency of identity and behavior of individuals desired by the current state in the various territories of oligarchic or totalitarian economic power. The Bureau of Guardians is One State's version of the FBI-CIA, KGB, Mossad, The General Directorate for External Security, Security Service M15, Ministry of State Security, et. al.

The current agencies of The Iron Heel have become pervasive and incidental, cooperative when necessary, using violence, repression of civil liberties, and torture exercised internationally to maintain the Iron Heel's Totalitarian and Oligarchic global powers. Economic systems have become arbitrary to the corporate synthesis of international high finance. George Orwell represented the situation in the "War is Peace" passage of *1984*: "All of the disputed territories contain valuable minerals…above all they contain a bottomless reserve of labor…reduced more or less openly to the status of slaves" (187). What Orwell understands through observation as the economic maintenance of The Iron Heel Oligarchy, reflects Randolph Bourne's statement, "But in general, the nation in wartime attains a uniformity of feeling, a hierarchy of values, culminated at the undisputed apex of the State ideal, which could not possibly be produced through any other agency than war's" (Bourne). Orwell concluded:

> The essential act of war is destruction, not necessarily of human lives, but of products of human labor. War is a way of shattering to pieces, of pouring into the stratosphere, or

sinking in the depths of the sea, materials which might otherwise be used to make the masses too comfortable, and hence, in the long run, too intelligent. (191)

Along with accomplishing nationalism and the internalization of false consciousness regarding common citizens and workers from the opposing nation now perceived as enemies (defined by the state as competitors for natural resources and cheap labor), the state also accomplishes the suspension or eradication of First Amendment rights and educational organizing methods that would reveal the schematic of the oligarchy or totalitarian regime and inspire imminent criticism and possible revolt. Zamyatin's passage on eradicating "Imagination" perceives the anti-state enemy as "the last barrier on the path to happiness. [...] The latest discovery of State Science: The imagination is centered in a wretched little brain node in the region of the *pons Varolii.*[2]Expose this node to three doses of X-rays—and you are cured of imagination" (173). In the U.S. the opioid and psychotropic pharmaceutical industry in part alleviates and facilitates the need for the *One State* or *Spaceballs'* X-ray or lazar procedure. Still, by eliminating massive numbers of the unemployed and the working class, which includes socially conscious men and women, war is also a method of minimizing the need for the threat stated by Wickson: "We will grind you revolutionists down under our iron heel..."

During the latter part of selecting, composing, arranging, and constructing "The Iron Heel Sequence," I communicated with a student struggling with the introspective component of an essay he was revising. To approach the introspective component he needed to declare why he personally was drawn to works of social consciousness that contain ethical criticism of the economic system. The poems he was analyzing, William Blake's "London" and Gil Scott-Heron's "The Revolution will not be Televised" are both poems critical of capitalism. I mentioned, if the exploitative and sinister part of the economic system is unacceptable to you personally, it should, for socially moral reasons be stated somewhere within an introspective

[2] The pons is also called the pons Varolii ("bridge of Varolius"), after the Italian anatomist and surgeon Costanzo Varolio (1543–75).[1] This region of the brainstem includes neural pathways and tracts that conduct signals from the brain down to the cerebellum and medulla, and tracts that carry the sensory signals up into the thalamus.

statement and recollection. For an example, I recounted the fact that my family was driven from Ukraine in the early 20th century by czarist-conceived and rapist and murder-directed Cossack (Death Squad) pogroms (massacres and incineration). When they arrived in the U.S. they were free from State and Mercenary violence but ended up in poverty working in sweatshops. Their stories of exploitation and economic struggle affected my worldview at an early age; so Tillie Olsen's poem, "I Want You Women Up North To Know," which focuses on the exploited garment workers living in impoverished conditions in Texas and elsewhere is a poem I personally feel close to because it introspectively reminds me that racism, sexism, and economic injustice is part of my family's experience, and the historical experience of underprivileged people and immigrants internationally. The poem also encourages me, in the sense that there were outspoken poets in the United States in the 20th century like Tillie Olsen and Gil Scott-Heron, and William Blake in 18th-19th century England who, because of their necessarily daring poems still continue to inform people of social and economic injustice and the struggle for human rights.

In the last chapters of *The Iron Heel*, there is vicious retaliation in the conflict London presents in "The Chicago Commune" battle where "The people of the abyss [from which] "the vampire society had sucked the juice of life"] had nothing to lose but the misery and pain of living. And to gain? —nothing, save one final, awful glut of vengeance" (207). So far, a collective reaction of a violence of this dimension has been avoided. Like the people of the United States that came out for the "Occupy Movement," the people that came out to protest "Black Lives Matter" were also protesting the impossible to live on wages, inadequate healthcare, college tuitions, threats to an already minimal social security system, dangerous work-place conditions, and police state brutality to all minorities and the vulnerable immigrants at our southern border. More than the Iron Heel metaphor, the facts display a thorough system of equivalent procedures for destructive results against specific targets.

Jack London's *The Iron Heel* is a historically indispensable novel of the early and ongoing international economic situation and the organization and rebellion of citizens oppressed by oligarchy in the early 20th century. The oligarchy is what we now understand as the 1%

totalitarian two-party leadership and corporate, militarily vested domination of the world economy that exists today. The 99% are struggling, perishing, organizing under and against the Iron Heel, the faces are indiscriminate, the current force, on either side, still intrepid, and driven.

Works Cited

Bourne, Randolph. "War is the Health of the State." https://www.panarchy.org/bourne/state.1918.html.

Orwell, George. *1984*. New York: Harcourt, 1977.

London, Jack. *The Iron Heel.* Westport: Lawrence and Hill, 1980.

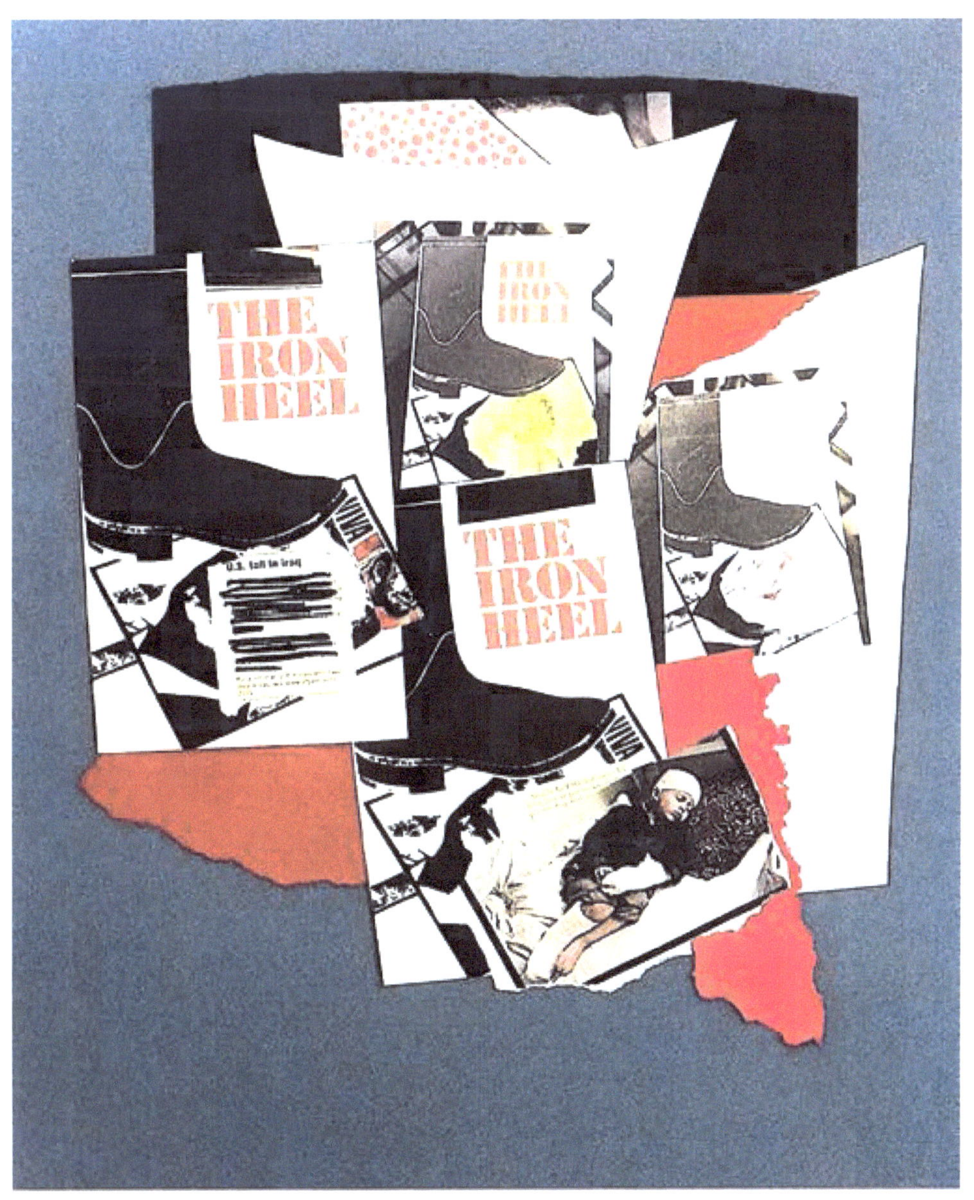

The Iron Heel Sequence 2. Photomontage, ink, and cut-outs. 2016.

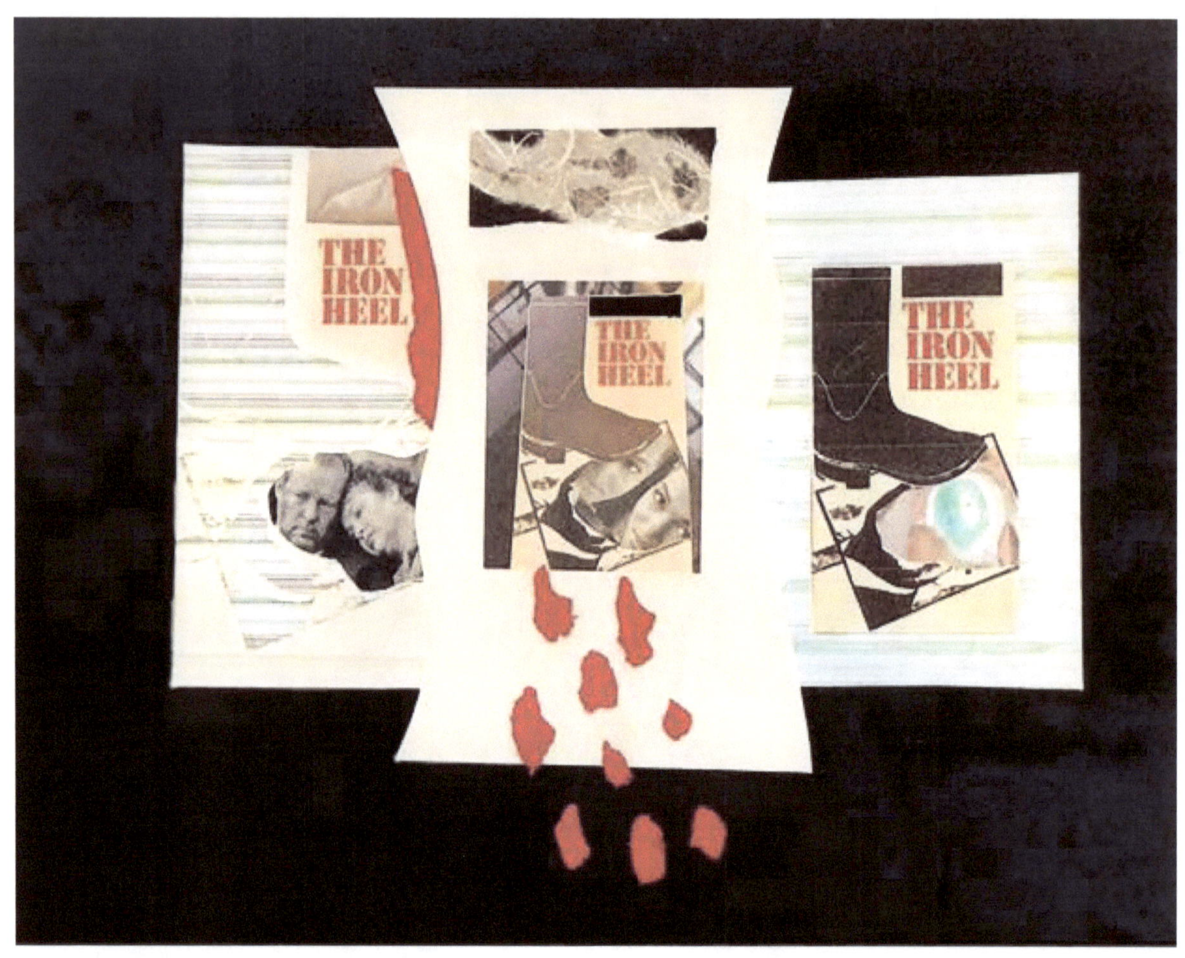

The Iron Heel Sequence 3. Photomontage, watercolor, and cut-outs. 2016.

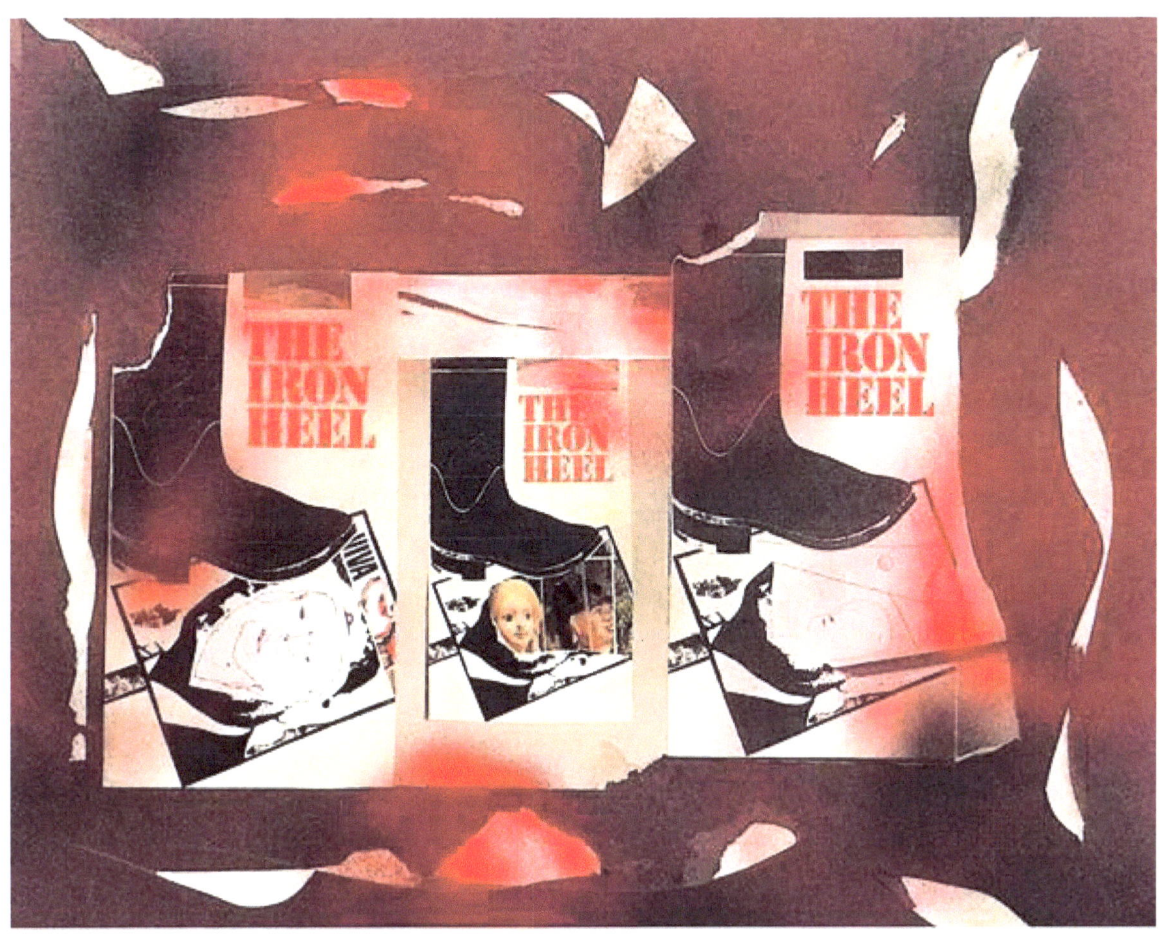

The Iron Heel Sequence 4. Photomontage, ink, spray paint, and cut outs. 2016.

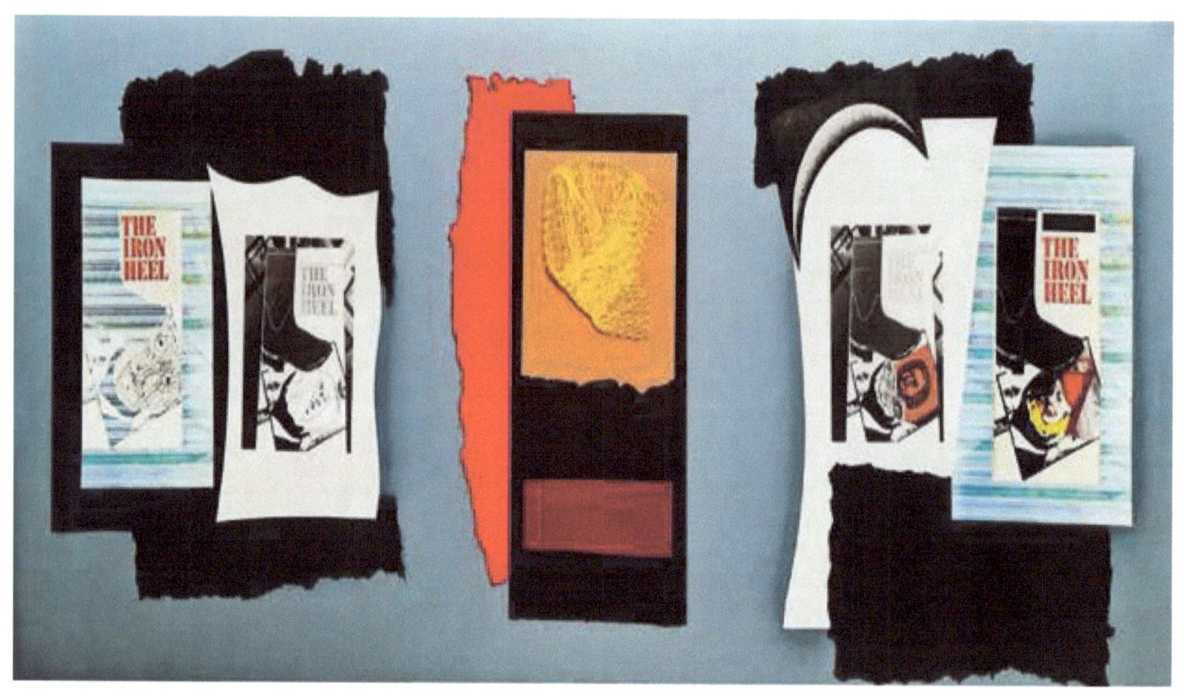

The Iron Heel Sequence 5 left detail. Photomontage, ink, and cut outs. 2016.

Gregor Samsa's Face

Nabokov went so far as to make diagrams of the fictional apartment
Gregor Samsa lived in as an insect but sketched no details for Gregor Samsa's face.
Why he didn't, he had his reasons. It couldn't have been a pleasant face, that insectization
of a man's lips, for instance. And we too would turn away from his mouth, the way we turn
from the dog's lick after yelling at him for nosing what some other dog left behind.
And there is something of a man being only worthy of garbage in Gregor Samsa
turned into an insect. I used to enter that world in rundown apartments when we worked
in maintenance. Some tenants offered us drinks in glasses not unclean but smeared from
so much ground into them—glasses they couldn't replace, drinks they really couldn't afford
to offer, or any of us to refuse. Driving back you would see the sage scrub above Hwy 1
where the insect-people had come from the colder cities to live in the open.
Gregor Samsa's face is the frozen face I saw in a subway dwelling, a face with hard red hair,
like Van Gogh's face of an injured saint, or fool, that all men are who have beards like the beard
I imagine on Kafka's character, and who don't know how to stop themselves from getting
swindled. As for Gregor Samsa: a man's beard caught on fire and, before they were evacuated,
three others came to warm themselves.

Shopping-cart globalism, Capital Homeless

I don't know the Homeless experience, my connection to the effects of their suffering is both blurred-out and distinct. Our connection is closest to one of the classical Italian or Dutch painters who understood universal suffering through the innumerable crucifixion victims they painted; or, to what Rembrandt saw, painted, and made drawings of in Amsterdam's Jewish Quarter, where he lived. In art, the modern human poverty archetype begins with a seventeenth century beggar Roelandt Savery made a drawing of, "Seated Man," his hat turned upside down to collect small change, his eyes drained against indifference; a socially critical, immemorial image, a face that will crease averted perception, commemorated by John Berger in his book, *Keeping a Rendezvous.*

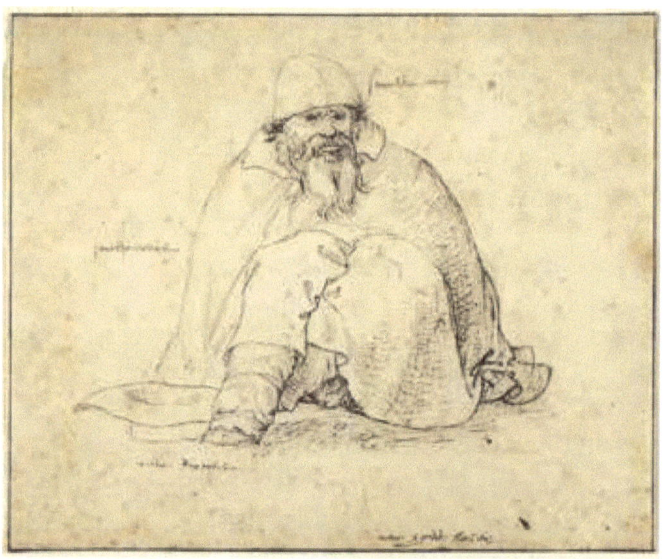

Roelandt Savery's "Seated Man."

I see the shopping-cart people when passing by, driving by, when I reckon, when I can hand over two dollars. Their images never exist outside the moment. If noticed. Something in the system drove them, something in the system conditioned and maintains the situation that led them to garbage food, garbage clothing, plastic bag storage, visible sickness, exposure, emotional disturbance. No recourse.

We don't know what solutions will result from the Supreme Court's "Grant's Pass" decision. It is a decision and ongoing problem systemic to capitalism, monarchy, oligarchy, and warlord tribalism. From the global economic system there's been a continuation of limited problem-solving. State indifference is policy. What direction did the United States, and the rest of the secure techno-industrial nations go after WWII, the beginning of the end of the completion of The New Deal? The opposite direction. Not from the two socially compassionate works, the Judeo-Christian *Sermon on the Mount* or Peter Kropotkin's *The Conquest of Bread*, but from The United Nations, Article 25 of the 1948 Universal Declaration of Human Rights:

> Everyone has the right to a standard of living adequate for the health and well-being of himself and of his family, including food, clothing, housing, medical care and necessary social services, and the right to security in the event of unemployment, sickness, disability, widowhood, old age, or other lack of livelihood in circumstances beyond his control.

But ethical-economic significance regarding systemic adjustment, like that expressed in UN Article 25, remains unapproached overall. The FeedingAmerica.org website notes: "More than 44 million people in the US face hunger, including 1 in 5 children. Millions of people in the US don't have enough food to eat or don't have access to healthy food (USDA's annual Household Food Insecurity in the United States report).

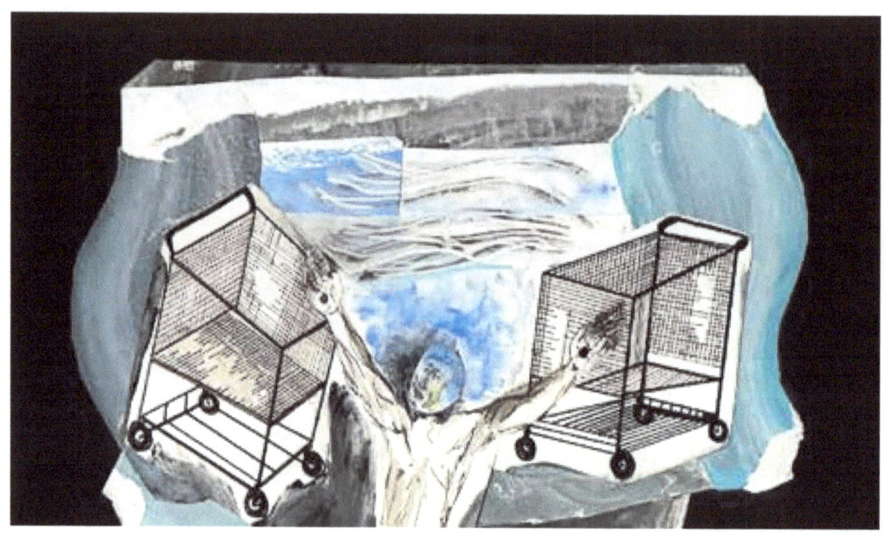

Detail from: Capital Homeless. Ink pen, graphite, watercolor, and cut outs. 2024.

In the U.S. there are approximately 653, 000 people experiencing homelessness; over 180, 000 in California. Euronews.com reports 330,000 in France. Of the mere 271,000 homeless in England, england.shelter.org.uk states: Almost two-thirds of people (63%) say that living in temporary accommodation has had a negative impact on their mental health. Half (51%) say that it has had a negative impact on their physical health. Two in five people (39%) say that living in temporary accommodation has made it harder to access healthcare appointments. The Lancet Regional Health Western Pacific web site insisted that "Homelessness is seldom a choice. Oftentimes, homelessness reflects the systemic failures that can result from social issues being dismissed or disregarded. Globally, approximately 1.6 billion people lack adequate housing, with 15 million more individuals being evicted on an annual basis. This situation is often profoundly worse in low- and middle-income countries like China. It is estimated that 300 million people in the country—home to 1.4 billion Chinese—are homeless."

The official figures include the shopping-cart people. Does it matter if you ignore official figures since what you understand as governing reliability, equity, dependability to transform the official figures won't happen? Where's the masses' contempt for official figures? Maybe there's not enough contempt to critically effect nobility? Ever. Monarchy and Oligarchy are secure. Why should it now suddenly affect them and their managers of economic markets? Isn't it deception and contempt to establish figures and make them official? By whose definition are figures official? Isn't it contempt for those they're certain have no educated question formulated or one possible to formulate. Some worn out pushing shopping carts. Some alive with no address. Or a car for an address. Working under the debtor's prison tower, the interview after the interview after the background check, after the drug test, the food stamp appointment, the shooting up before waiting in line for Veteran's Benefits, disability small change in the nobility-tilted system. World leadership believes they express sincerity without being self-serving. Maybe there's an extracted area in the logic of that part of their minds. Doesn't mockery of hypocritical officials and their figures, their UN Article 25 corrupt-athon, confirm pessimism as satire-entertainment to anyone disgusted by ethical insignificance? Don't we still have nobility's armed response, their surveillance down to the toothpick, their International Monetary Meth-Lab of Labor Nobility Consortium kicking targeted unionists and workers' asses? That Globalism. In part, NAFTA's exploitative bottom-line success. Their appetites. It's a dictatorship. What if it is a dictatorship? Ralph Nader's father defined the situation as "socialism for the rich." To the homeless, the slave labor class, and the working-class, the twenty-first century is a world of plantations-Great Depression era continuation of the twentieth.

The problem has not always been recorded in Modern art. In painting, the otherwise remarkable French Modernist, Ferdinand Leger omits the destitute French veterans of WWI, the poor, and the visible struggles of workers and families that German artists Kathe Kollwitz, Otto Dix, and George Grosz perplexed into memorable imagery. To a contemporary list of quotidian elements, to Leger's utopic work sites, picnics, cyclists, and machinery, we should now add the population living in Russian sewers; affordable housing in parking lots, the freeway underpass, and subterranean garages; continuous smog drift, unendurable traffic; neofascist demonstrations; multiple agricultural workers' families inhabiting one-room apartments; and the Homeless sidewalk homesteads, cheap tent life, parked shopping carts, and then the cleansed site of shopping carts disappeared by city clean-up crews.

There are reasons to fear or be apprehensive about the reality of being a nomad, or worse, a physically or mentally sick nomad in the twenty-first century no man's land. For anyone not incapacitated, who sees through the transient comfort of still making purchases and paying rent or mortgages, that is, the majority who have jobs or pensions but do not own islands or have access to vacation homes on remote islands or underground bunkers—the shopping-cart people present a living rehearsal, prelude-reality, an alternate world, after one of the wars, climate catastrophes, severe economic breakdowns to come.

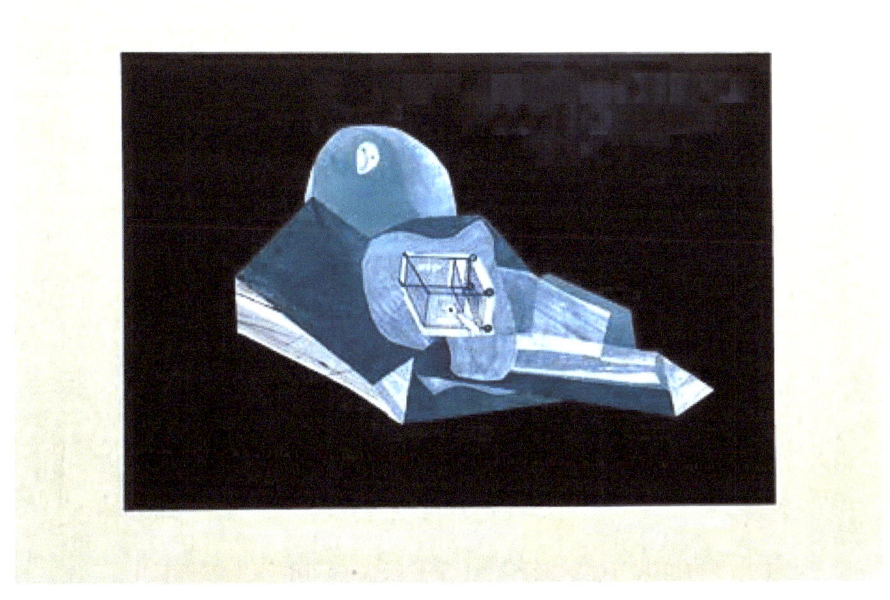

Shopping cart tossed into LACMA tar pit. Ink, watercolor, and cutouts. 2024.

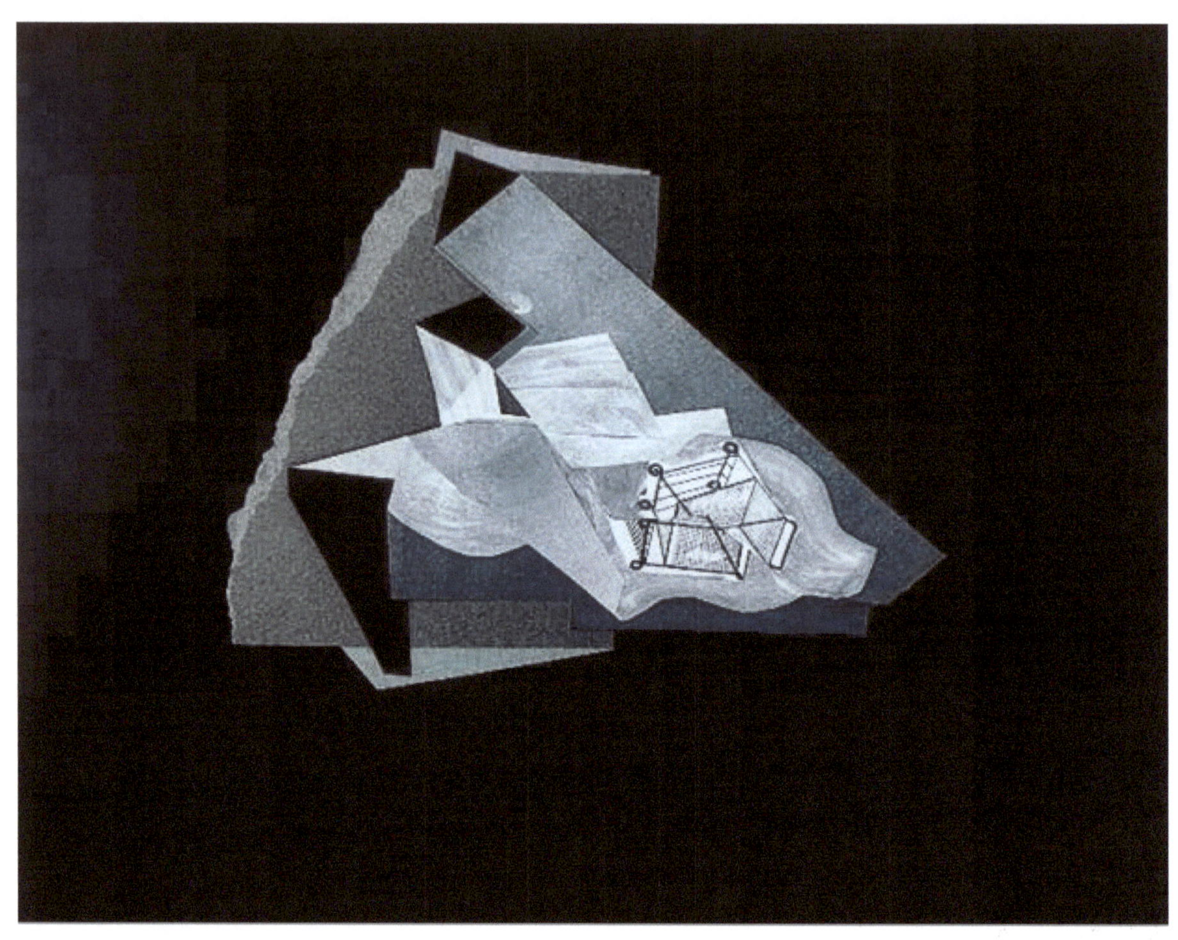

Copulating Shopping carts. Ink, watercolor, and cutouts. 2024.

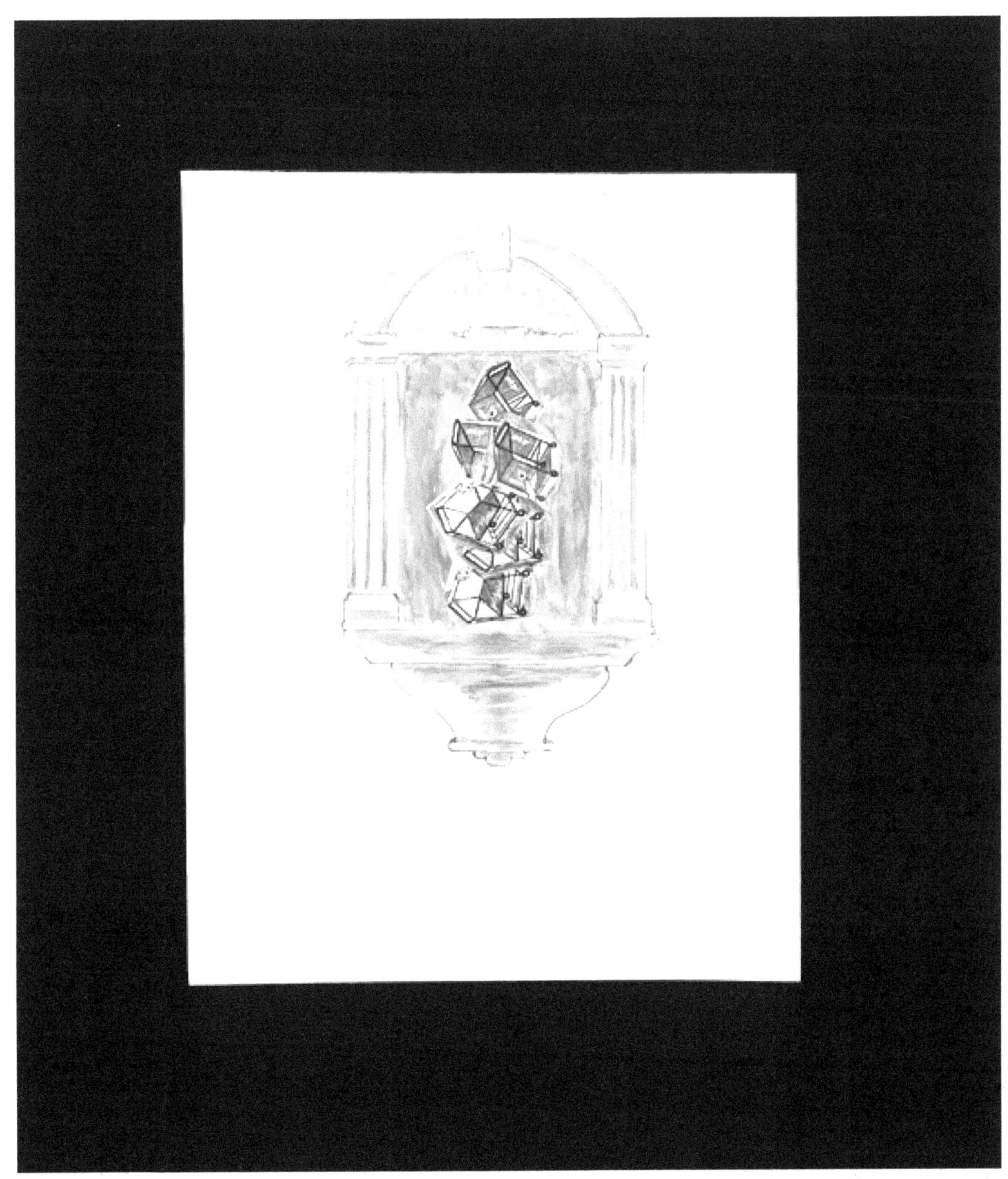

Shopping carts, classical niche. Pen and brush, ink, and cut-outs. 2024.

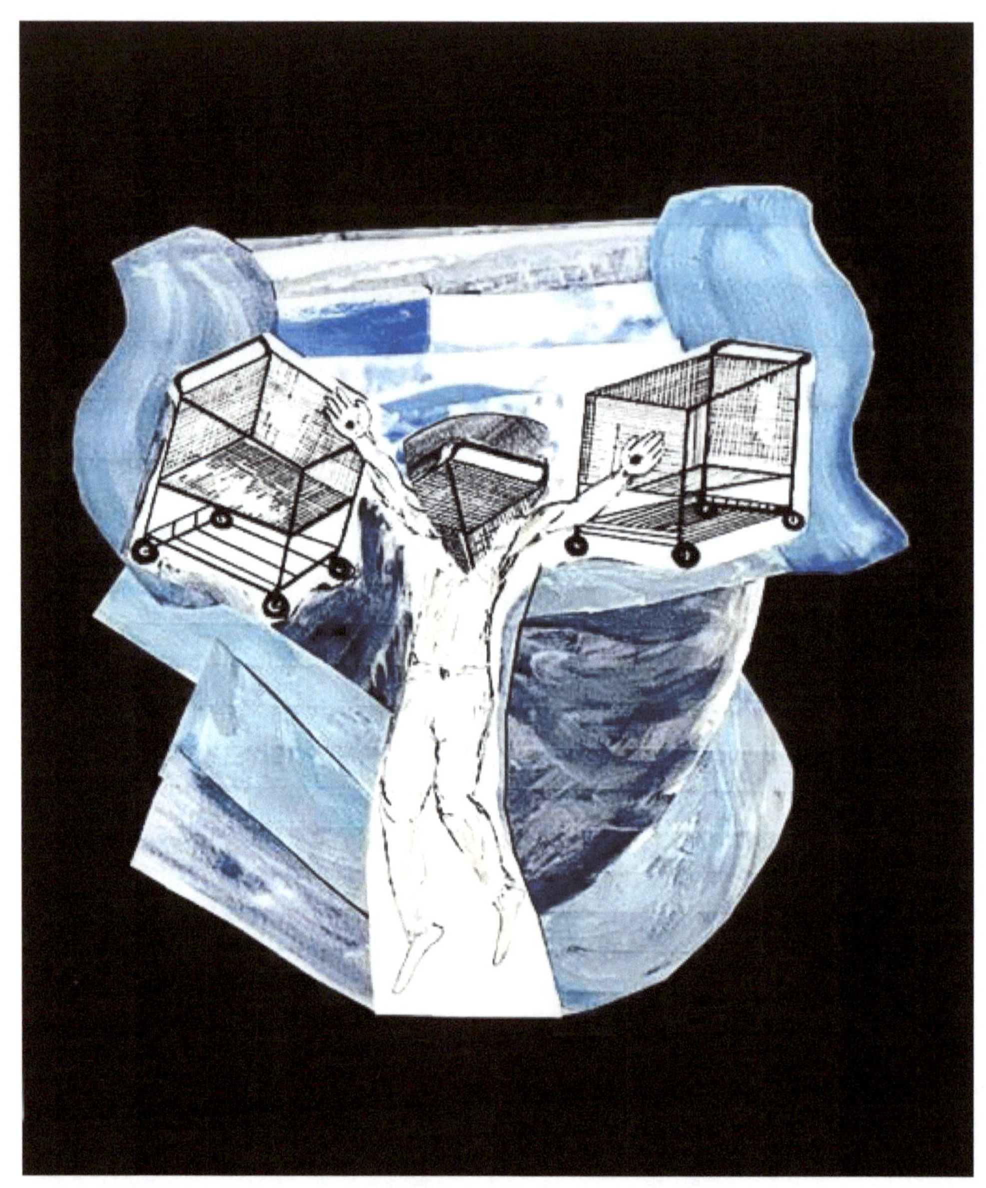

Crucified shopping cart. Ink pen, graphite, and watercolor. 2024.

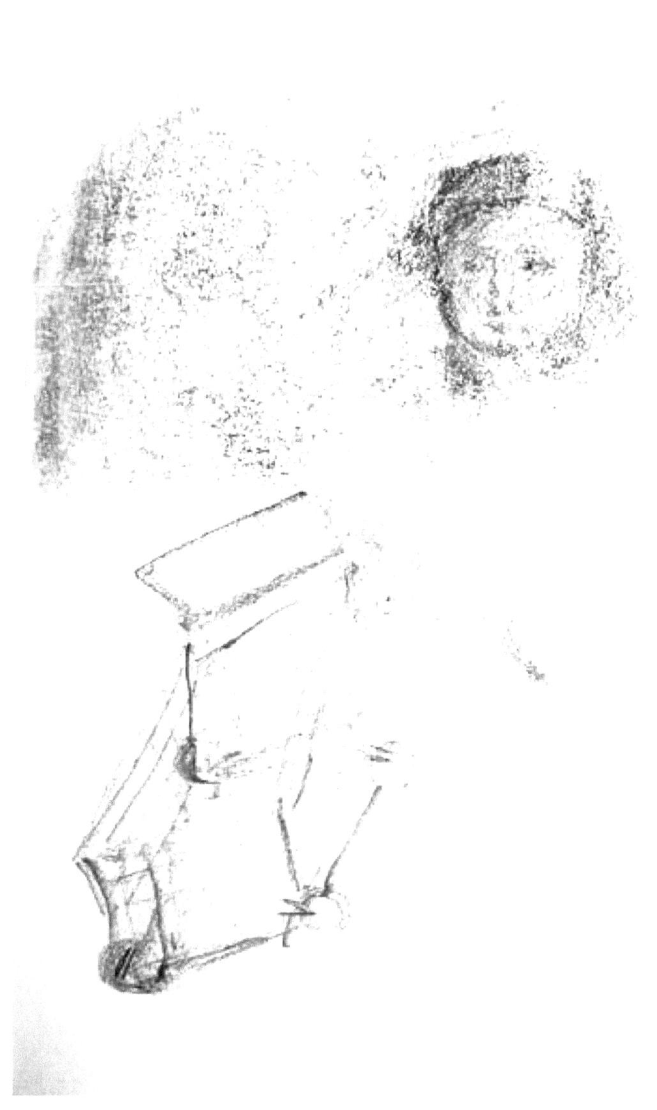

Empty cart off Moon Alley, Santa Cruz CA. Graphite. 2024.

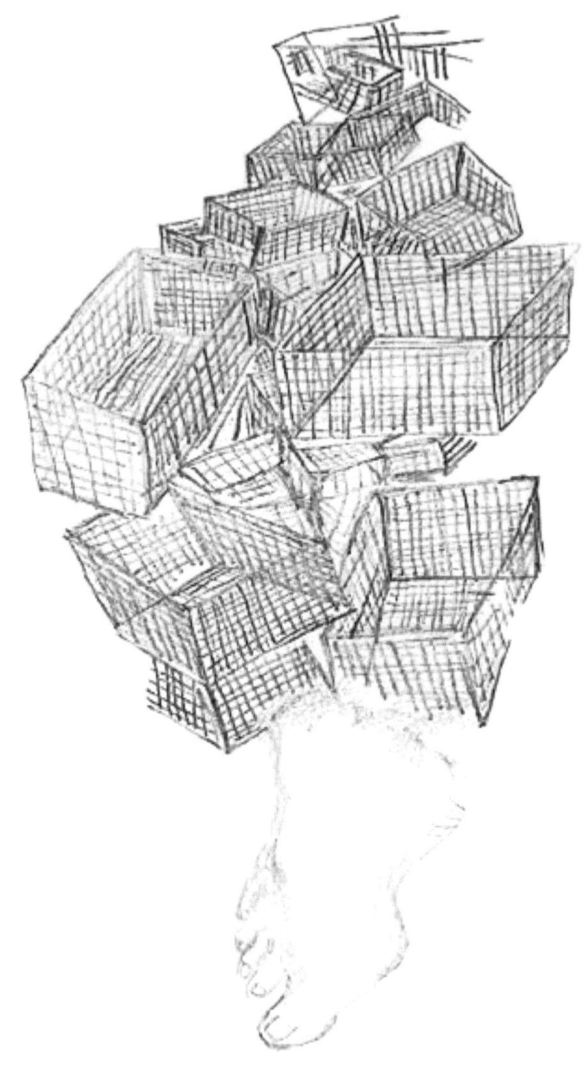

Recycled shopping carts supported by right foot. Satire 1. Ink and graphite. 2024

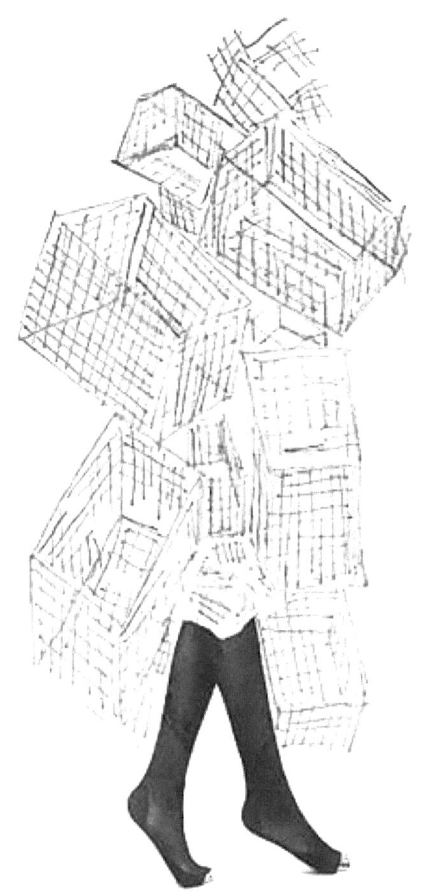

Shopping cart femininity. Satire 2. Ink and photomontage. 2024.

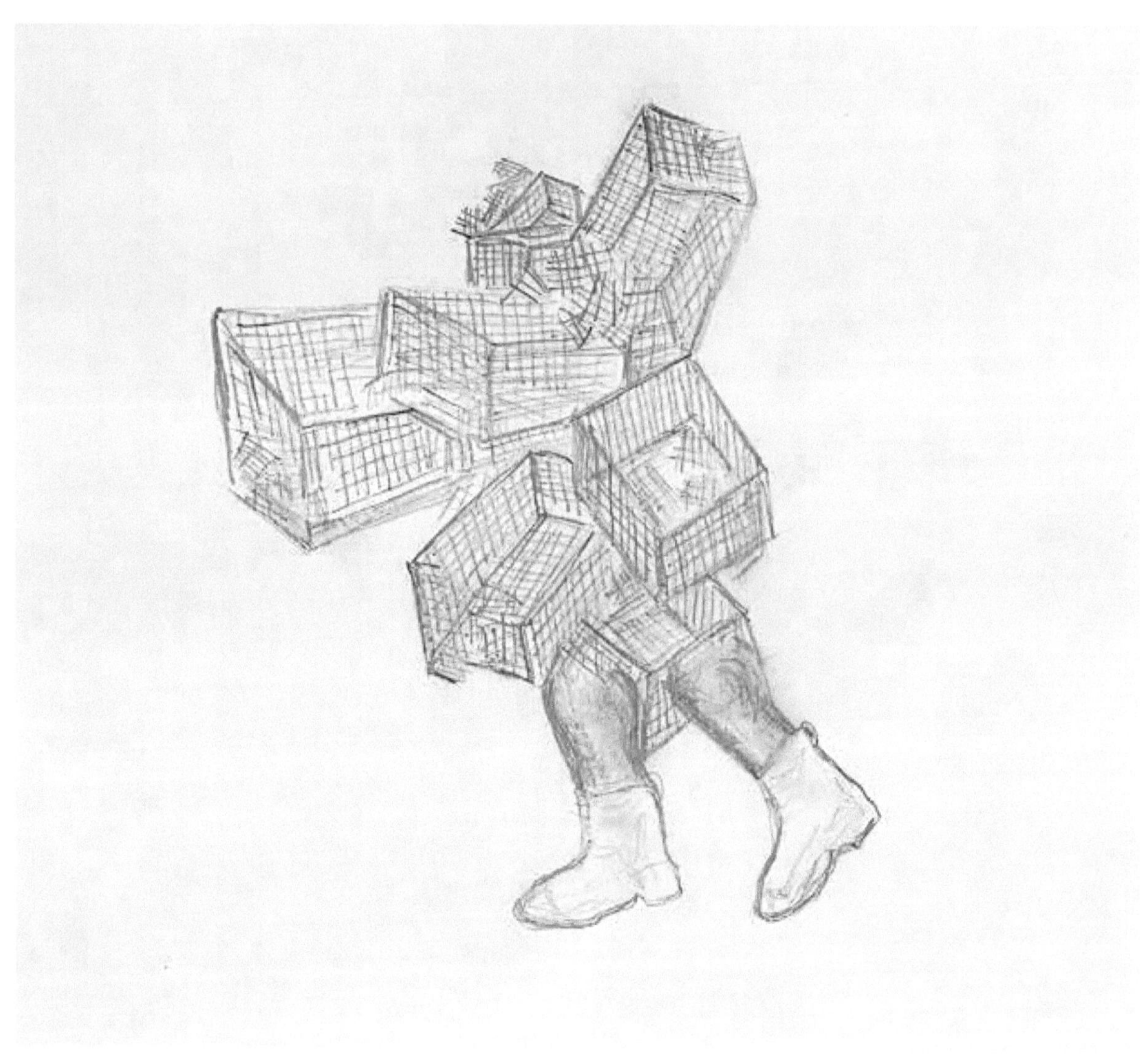

Shopping cart action figure. Satire 3. Ink and graphite. 2024.

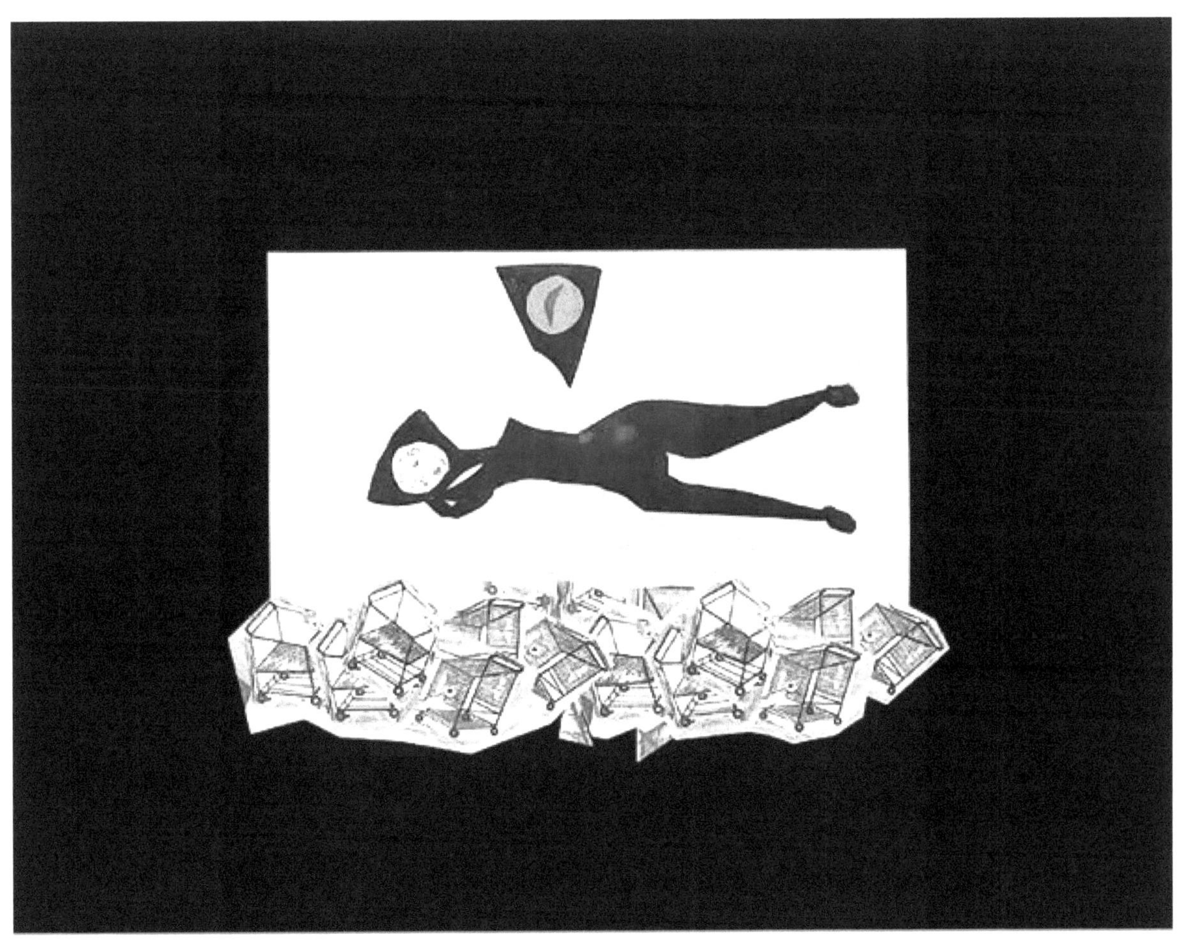

San Lorenzo River of shopping carts. Ink and cut-outs. 2024.

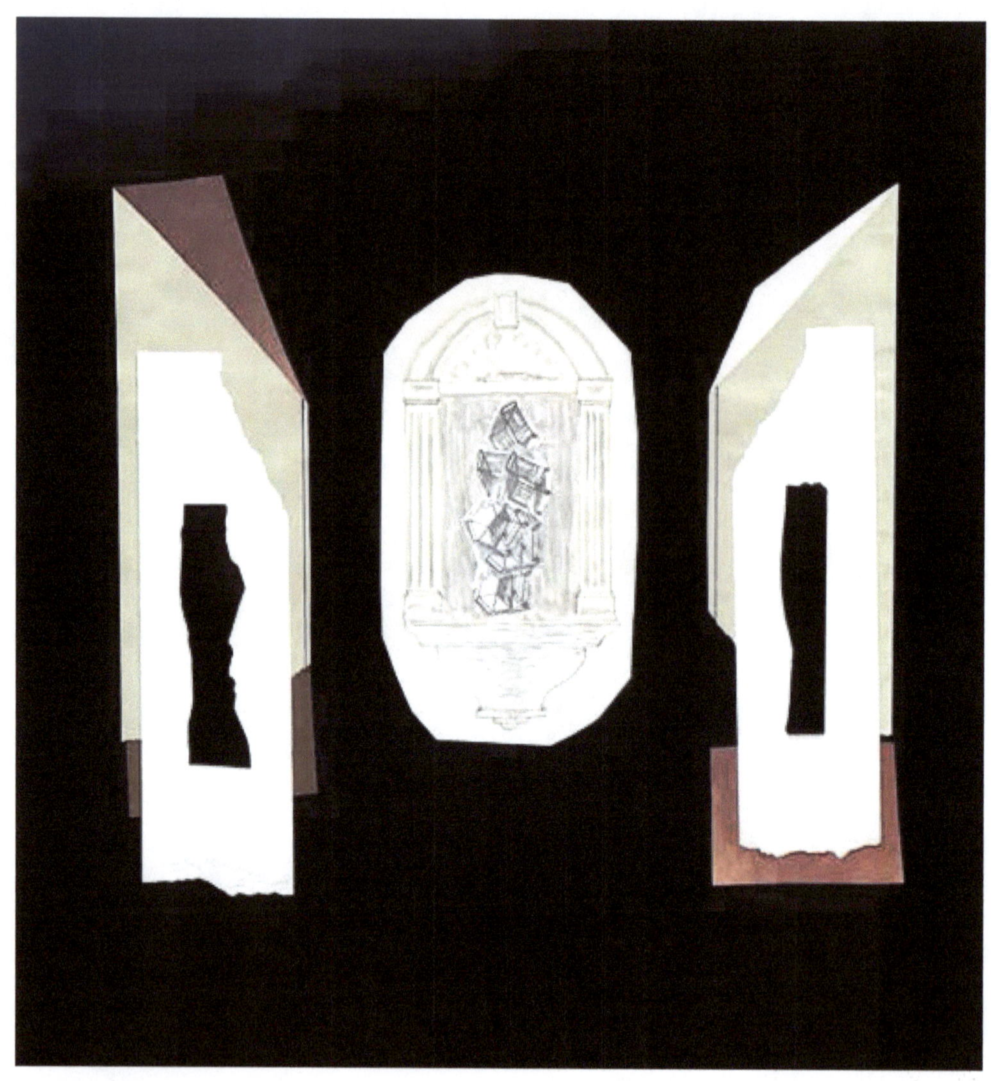

Shopping cart, classical niche, fantasy columns. Ink, acrylic, and cut outs, collage. 2024.

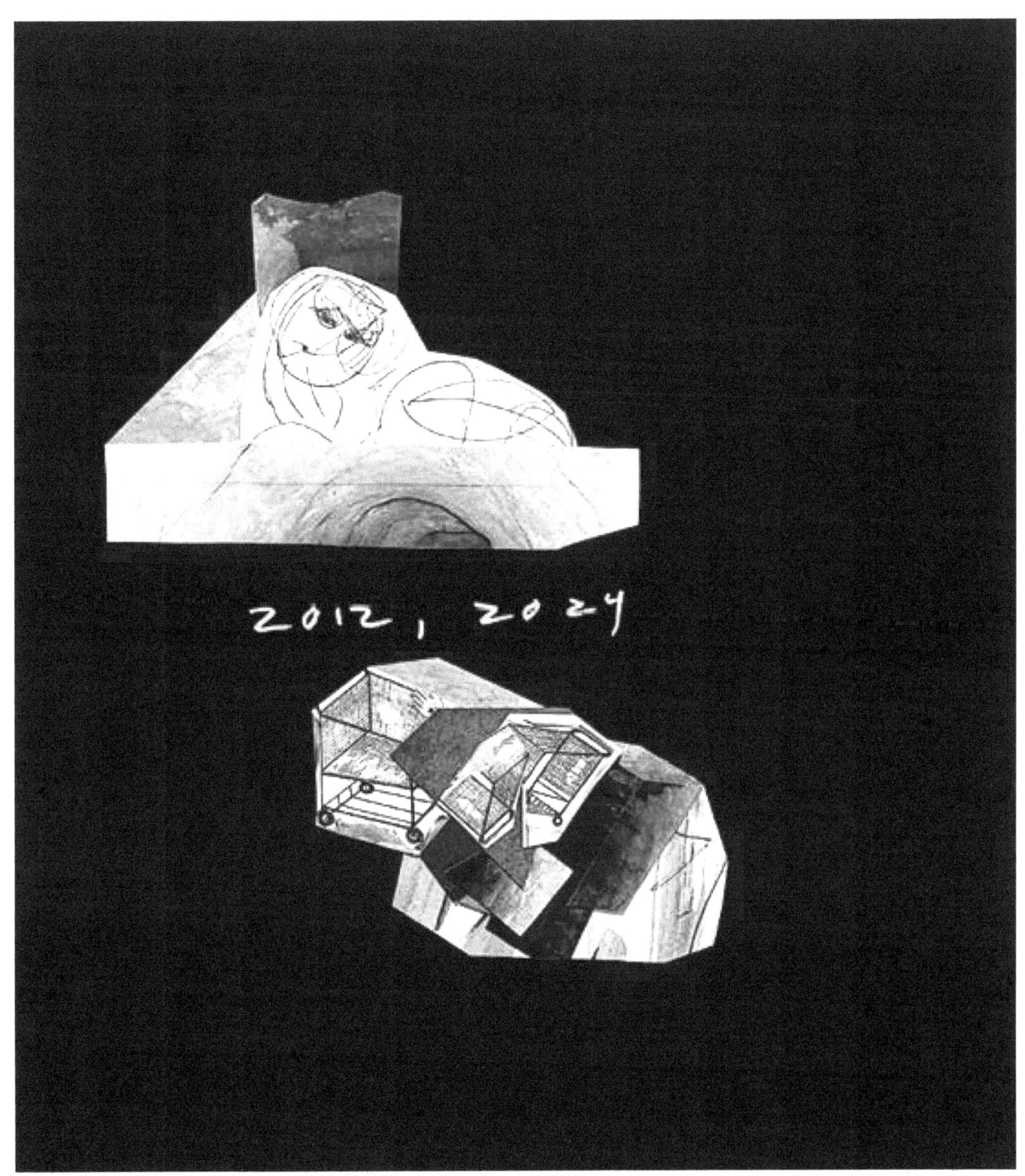

Title in the image. Ink, acrylic, cut-outs, collage. 2024.

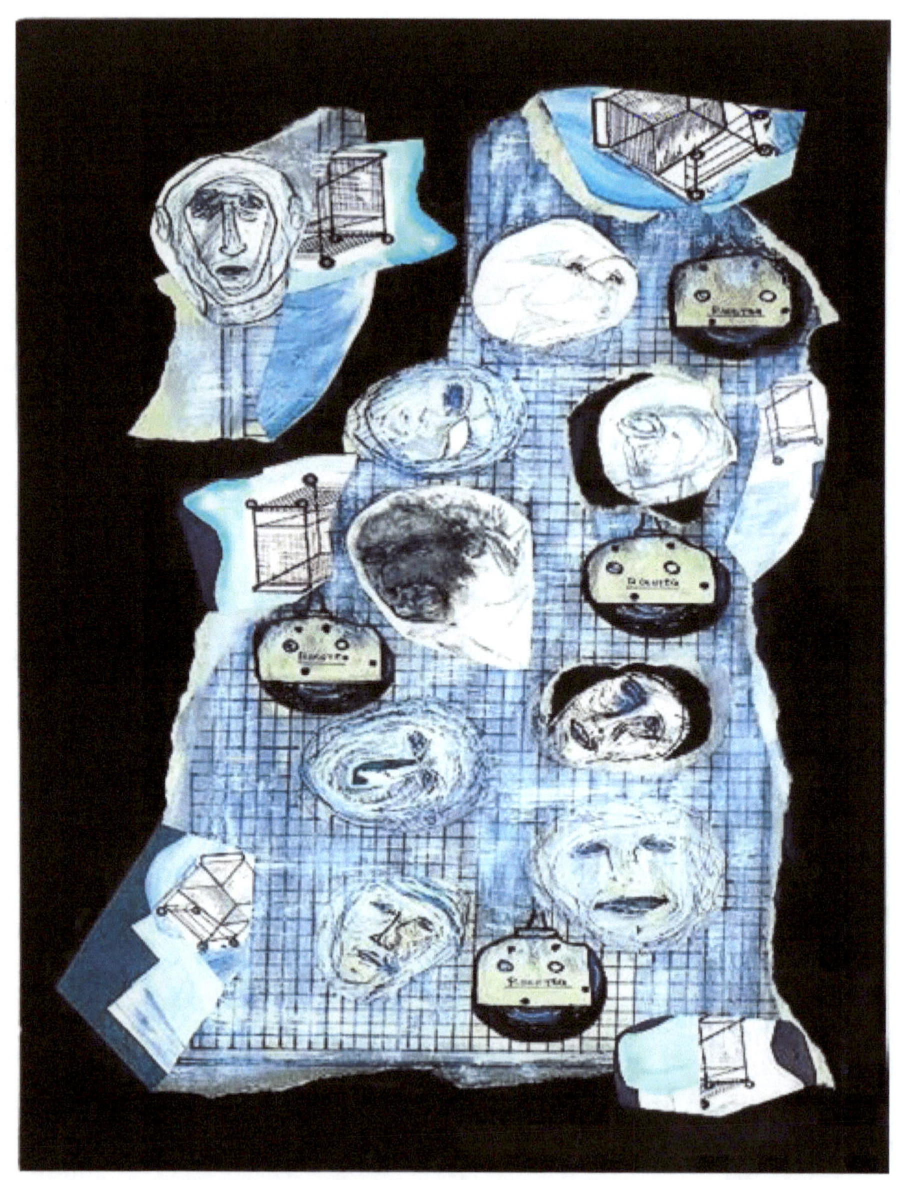

Nine heads, four wheel-locks, bottom tray, shopping cart.
Ink, acrylic, cut-outs, collage. 2024.

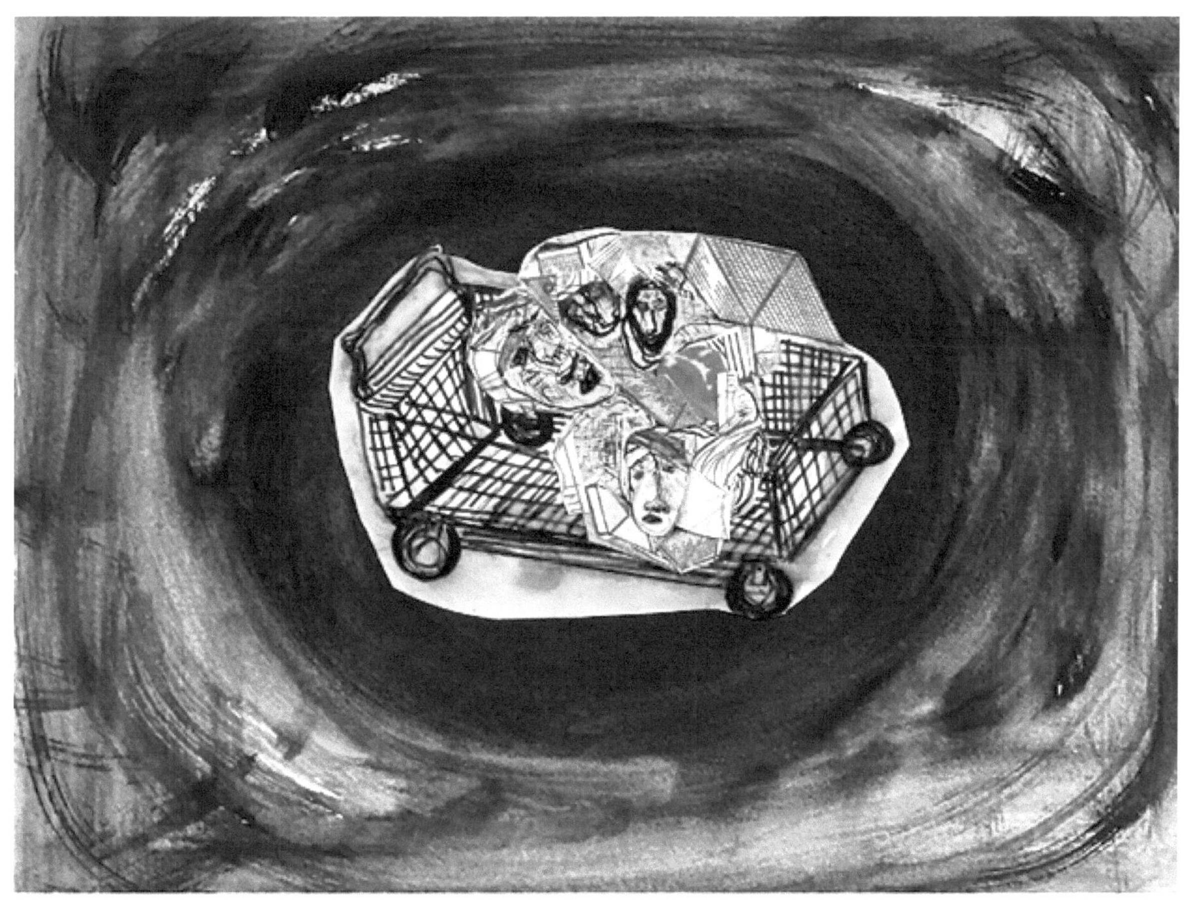

Heads, shopping carts, wreck outside CVS. Ink, watercolor, cut-outs, collage. 2024.

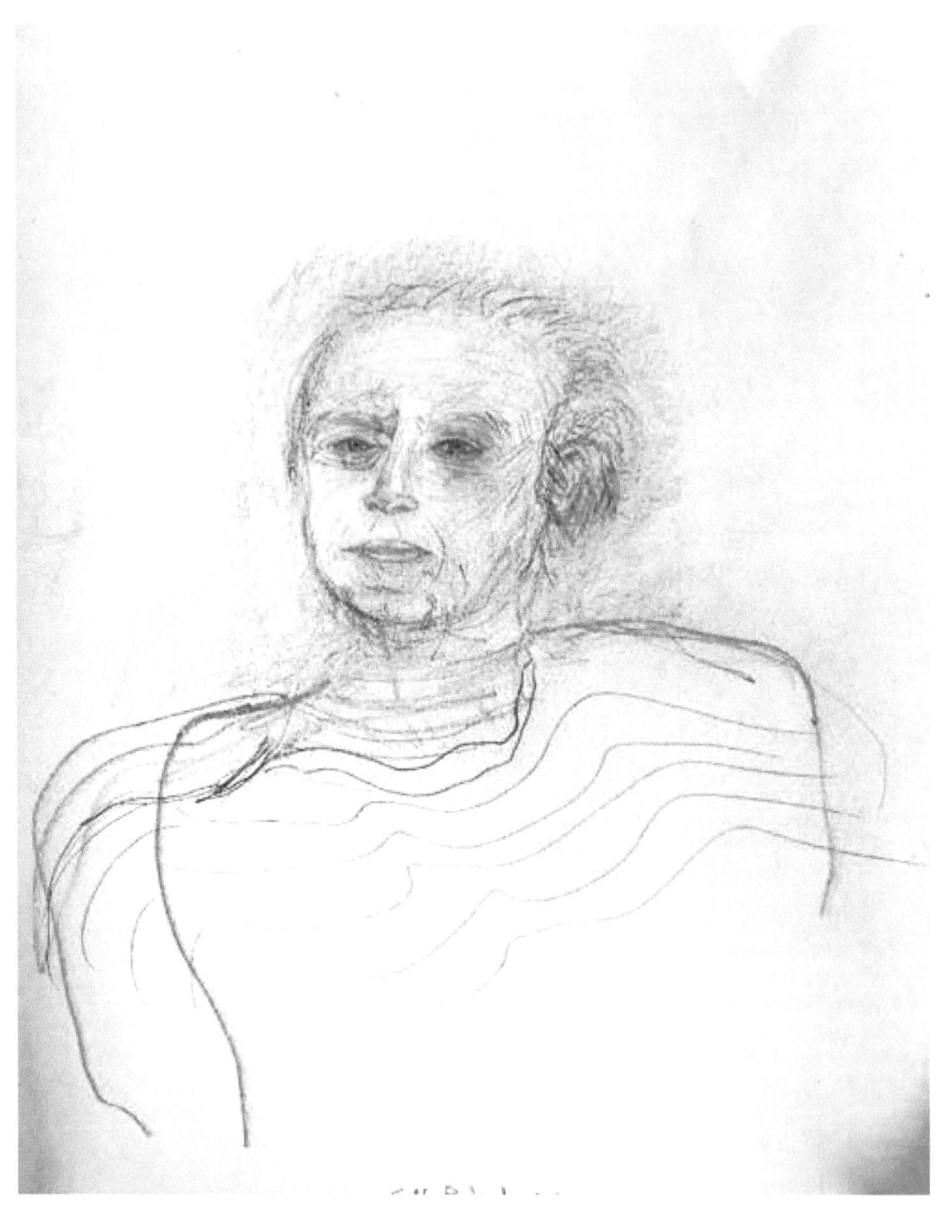

Man facing homeless camp. Graphite. 9 x 12. 2023.

Monologue Poem: Under the worlds' leadership there's a lot of shopping carts,[3]

ants licking dead snakes dry, the cancer of obedience, a septic pit for the unrequited unemployed,

under the world's leadership there's a lot of Haitians eating cookies held together with dirt, an unbearable victims' aura to multiple races, unmovable bowel crust and toxic meat syndrome, Asshat media pundits surplus, hoppity rapidly following hippity, workers constructing Dracula's athletic shoes...

there's a lot of armament producing thugs under the world's leadership, landlord dickheads, derangements that don't finally compute, cunnilingucide, *toilet injustice,* drugs to endure consciousness, cantors of mishegas, expulsifiers in general,

no one taking you up on your offer under the world's leadership, nowhere left to buy sour dough on a stick, no one to distinguish and enforce ethical reasoning shaping acts of two kinds, ones that enhance the well-being of others—that warrant our praise—and those that harm or diminish the well-being of others—and thus warrant our criticism,

under the world's leadership there's a twelve-foot reality bronze sculpture village man-village-village-boy hands held walking a Cretan village square monument commemoration complete rounding-up males aged ten to sixty World War Two grave dump village 800, 713 on the list, in the permanence of that which happens...

under the worlds' leadership
labor emperors determine the lunch break, cigarette break, overtime schedule, non-increase of wages, expendable holidays, the entire Asshole Brigade,

there's a lot of Blackwater Felugia My Lai Bailout broth with the bones inside of it, with the purse inside of it, with the child's nose inside of it
under the world's leadership

[3]The poem plays out of Allen Ginsberg's poem, "Under the World There's a Lot of Ass" (*Mind Breaths*, City Lights Books, 1978).

there's an archeology of whip handles, explosives inside toilet tanks, reinstate the draft enthusiasts, international military gang rapists, political Emoticon designers making their Emoti-cackling behind our backs, mass murder at music and garlic festivals,

there's a lot of self-dug graves, sagittal sores, uncockered and still declitoral spaniels, one last metric ton of Mountain Dew dispersed in the enigmatic collective fertility dream,

there's a lot of disappearing egg receptacles, spermatozoa sparkulation defects, emotionoscopies, tech-dreckology, waste pipes leaking under suicide-bombed abortion clinics, the dirty feathers tradition, the sing and mate till you dry up tradition

under the worlds' leadership

there's a multiplying assassination battalion academy industry, oligarchs' multiple compounds, five-hundred thousand to one million plant and animals' species facing the extinction catalogue,
there's a lot of unripe uranium, ocean plastic pollution set to grow fourfold by 2050, sleep harassment, invisible bowties, lost hair implants, sexy bags of books, discreditors of sentient thinking, disappeared labor organizers, disappeared protesters against the worlds' leadership,

under the world's leadership

there's a lot of war criminals, extinction criminals, dyslexias, analexias, melancholectomies, DOA identities, the oblivionated, the depresstapated, and exasperized, not always with someone to rub your own foot, your symbiotic pressure points, your direct hope and negative feeling for the situation to end under the world's leadership extinguishing my Retsina dream meditation marriage sleep refuge peace, of a limited entanglement here.

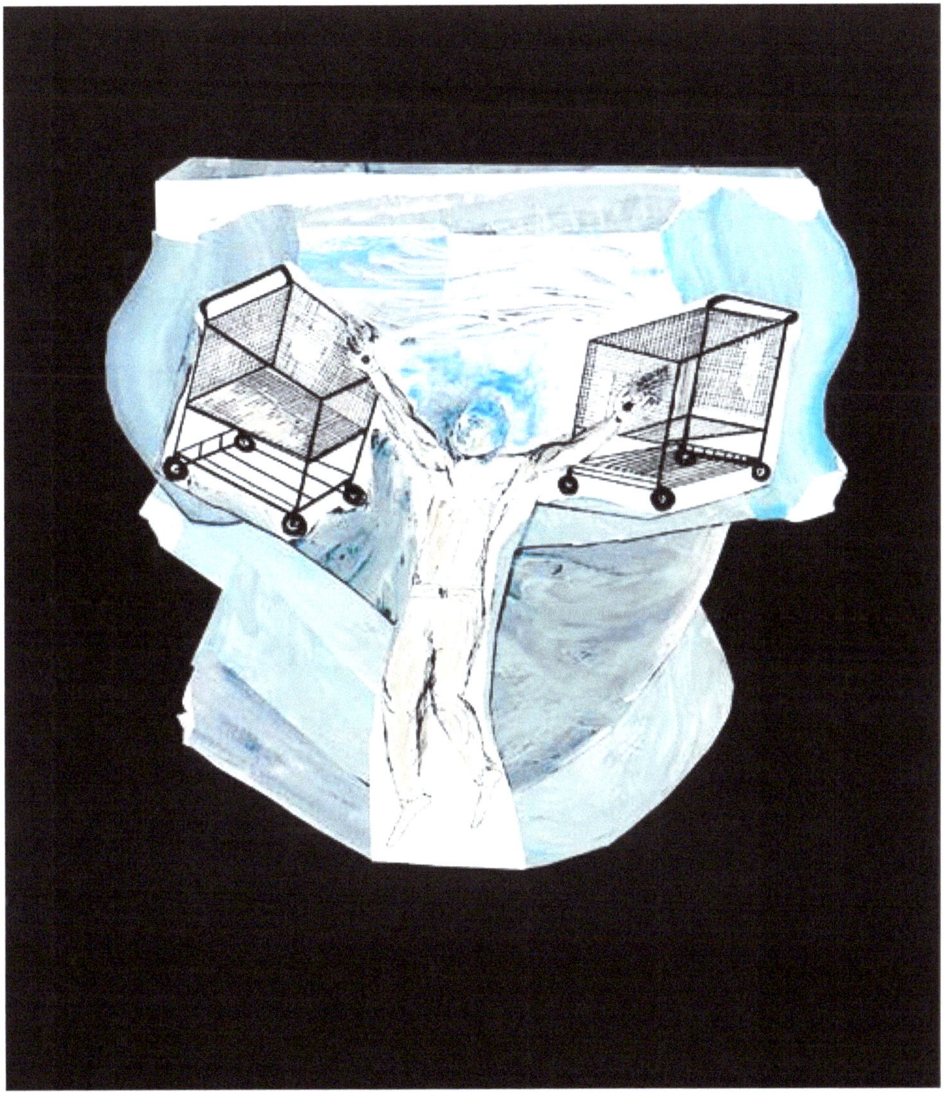

Capital Homeless, outside 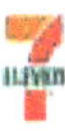 Ink, Cut-out., Collage. 16 x 20. 2024

To the Veras, to Nazim Hikmet

The stove and Vera stirring the broth in his mind
in the prison cell hut of his blood. You figure out your own light company
in there. You see the stove without the name of a country stamped on it.
Somebody's making an ode to broth on that burner or an ode to cast iron
or the clay of China, to brick and mortar, to the clothes you live in, the stove
that will do all the way to Guantanamo, because Guantanamo updates him.

The ode is to Vera's thick hand lifting the ladle private in a husband's fantasy
or a wife's fantasy, a bone broth prison fantasy ode to Vera setting down the soup
bowl and the common fact of dipping the spoon, a poet making his inquiries
dipping

a spoon to the phrase of musical immediacy, Django Reinhardt sullen or sweet
Jim Hall, to the plant life of the mind some poets water into a salvaged mood,
to the surge at the end, half of what's rare undefined until the end.

Ode to the prisoner working in there, the sensations and fantasy life in there
twenty years after getting locked up for a book of poems accused of inciting the
Turkish people to revolt. That it were still true for us now, the easily deceived and
betrayed he said he wrote for, whatever subway or bus stop you wait at you
just have to look around.

Intruder Sequence. Iraq, Afghanistan, Gaza, Israel, Ukraine, Russia, etc.

The works in the sequence, "Captured intruder, conflicted mercy, more cruelty, enigma," are not in themselves anti-war representations, but rather presentations of the drama, and personal responses to, violent aggressions and the instinct to vengeance.

In a recent poetic monologue, my speaker makes the third-person commentary:

> He feared humans that secrete or stiffen when they hunt. How can you not fear the species uncommitted to save the last of the honeybee species? A repine-aholic species. A species without the skill in time. He feared urethral interrogations and the follow orders mentality. A water violation to health, petrochemical slum species. He feared the fact Simonides, Hobbes, and Lorenz are right: only the dead know the end of aggression
>
> (from "Voicer 18: Surveillaspeak").

In tandem with the political ethics embodied in my writings and in the courses I developed as a Literature, Critical Thinking, and Creative Writing Professor 1991-2022, my engagement is embedded in a life-long meditation on my grandparent's survival of pogroms in early twentieth century Ukraine, loss of relatives in Stalin's Gulags, and my father's disease and PTSD from the Pacific War, WWII.

These works were begun at the beginning of the Russian attacks on Ukraine, continuing on to the Palestine-Israeli atrocities, Sudan, etc.

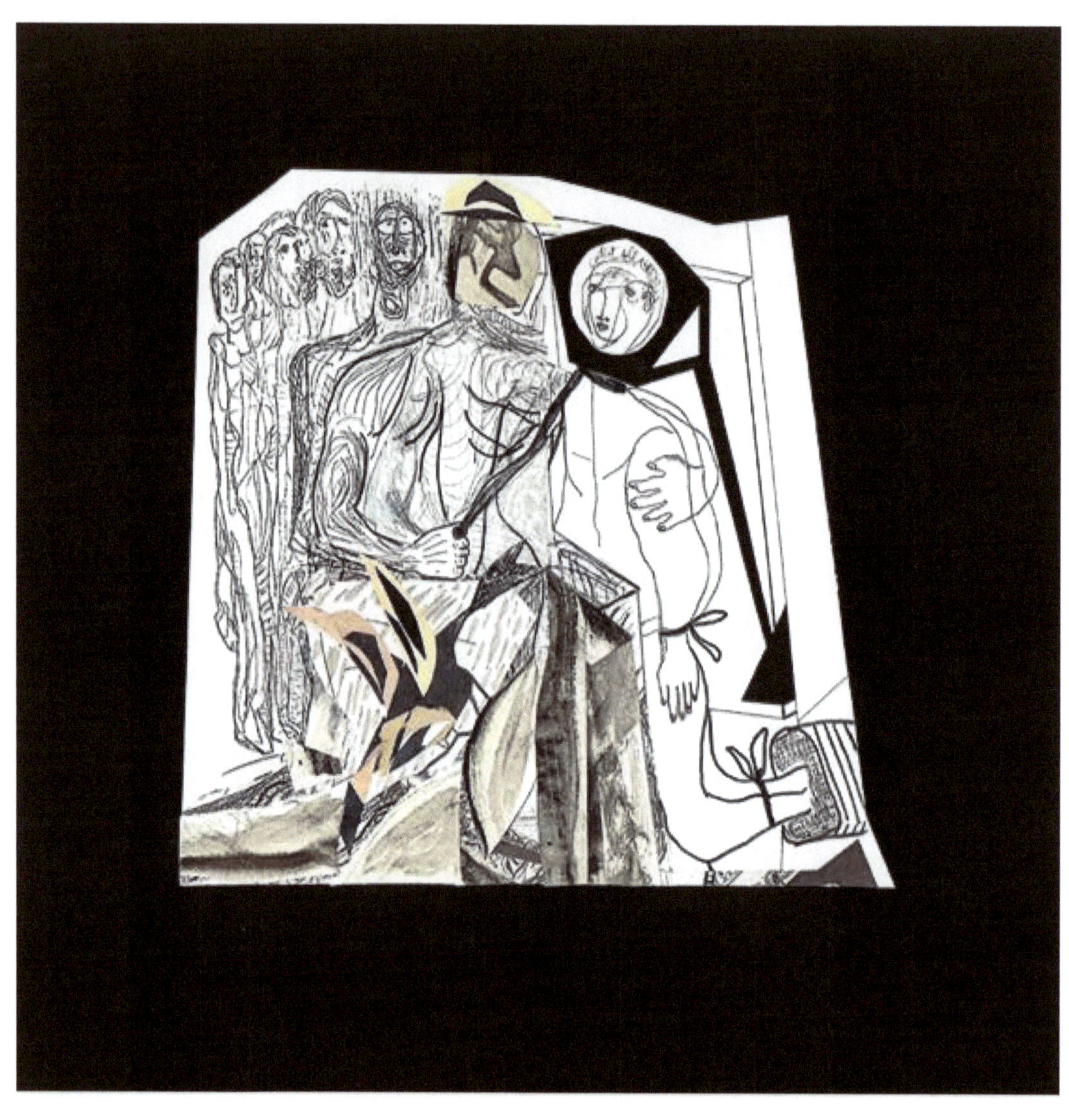

Captured intruder 1, guardian bird. Brush and ink, cut-out, collage. 2023.

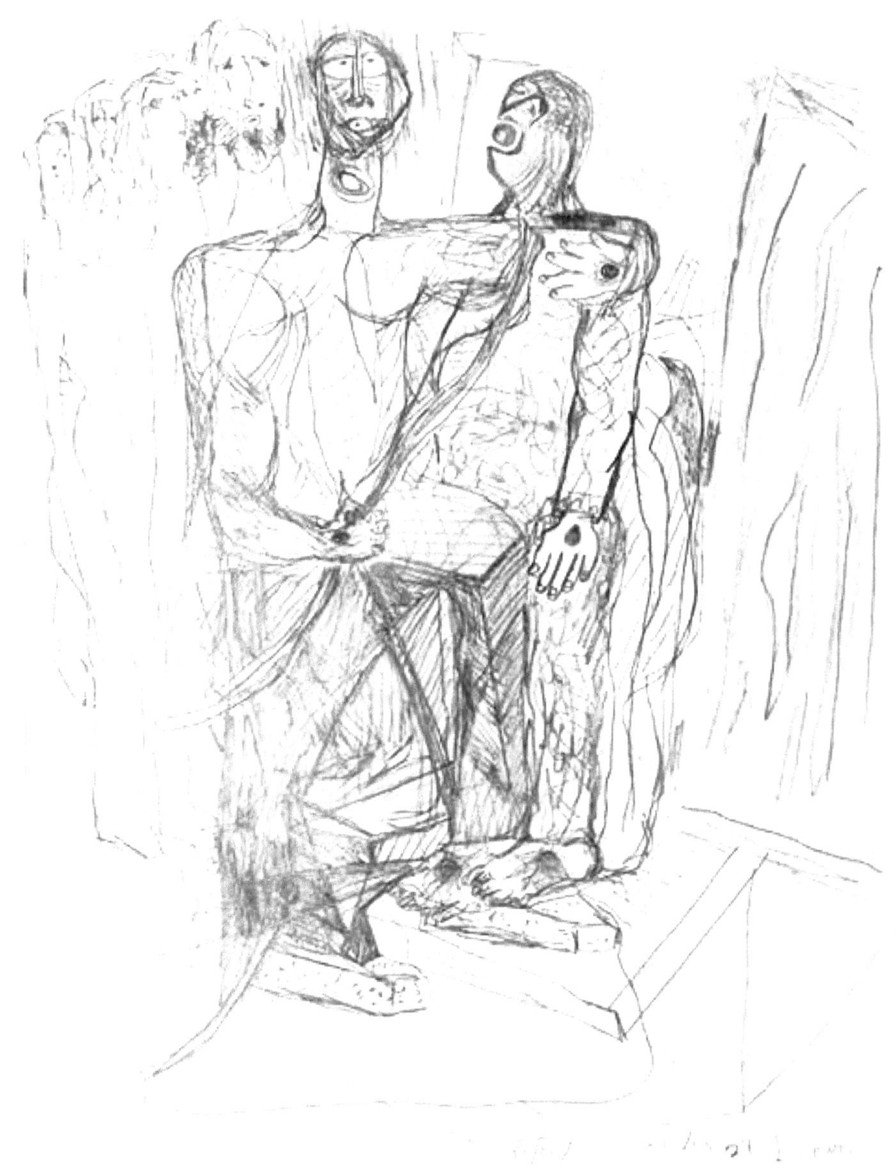

Captured intruder 2. Graphite. 2023.

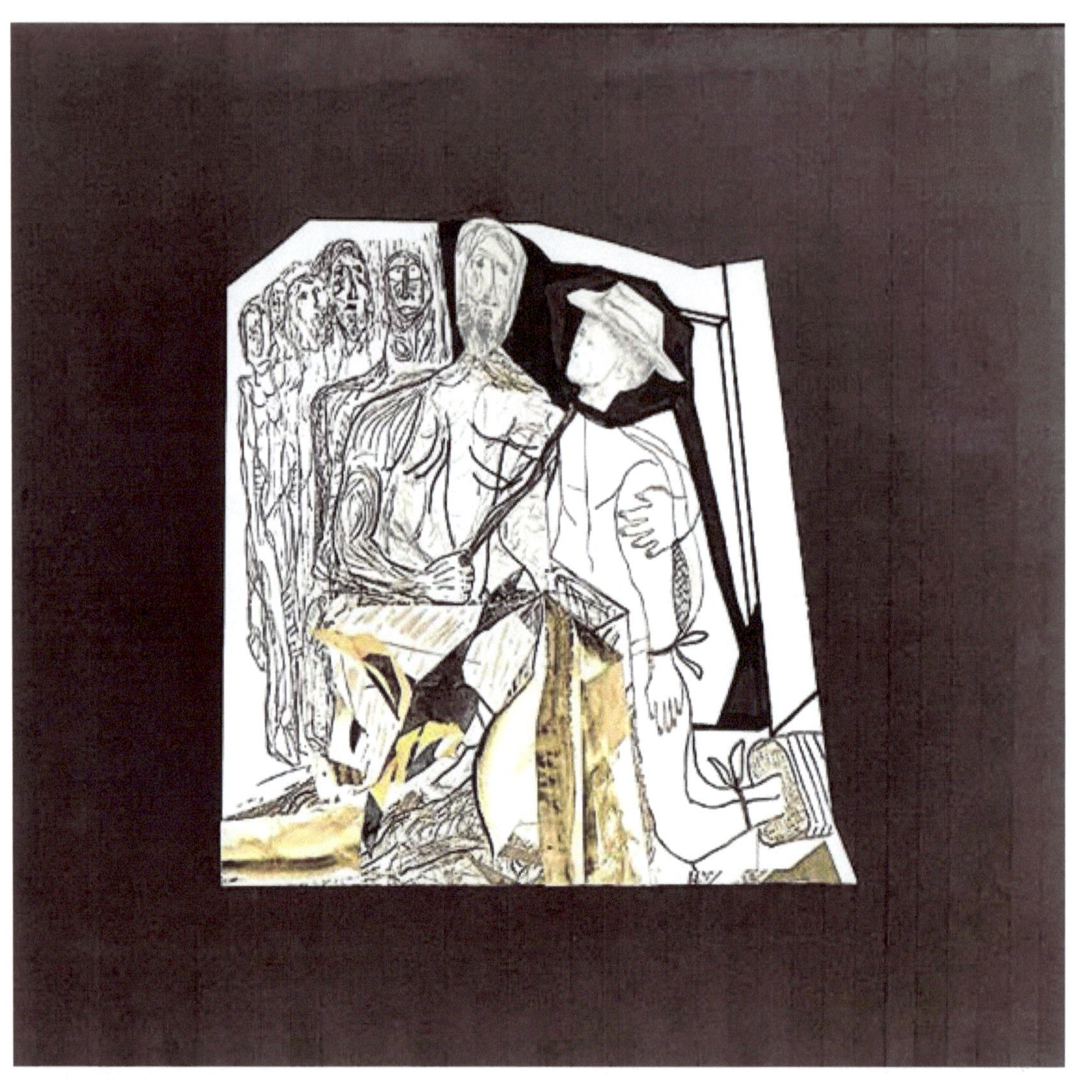

Captured intruder 3. Watercolor, ink, cut-out, collage. 2023.

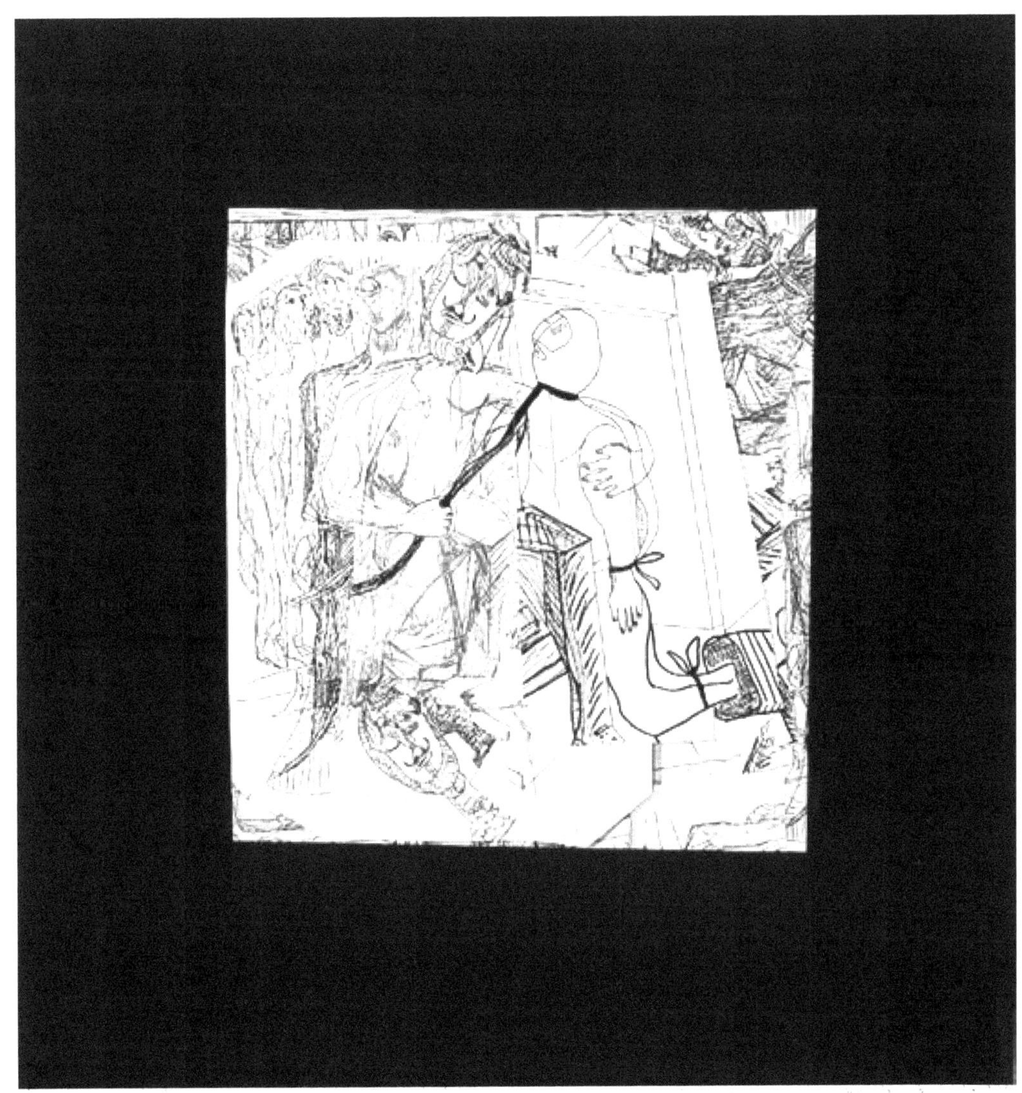

Captured intruder 4. Ink. 2023.

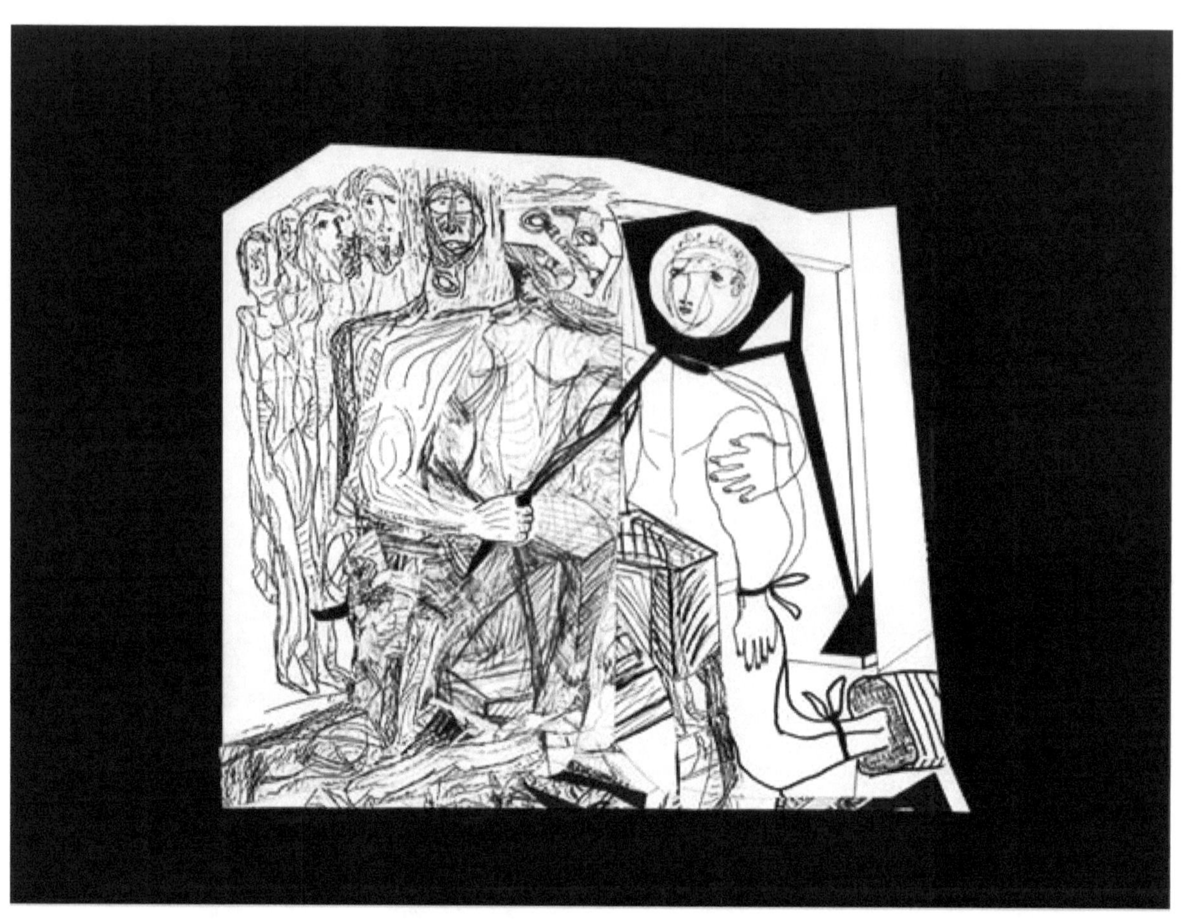

Captured intruder 5. Ink. 2023.

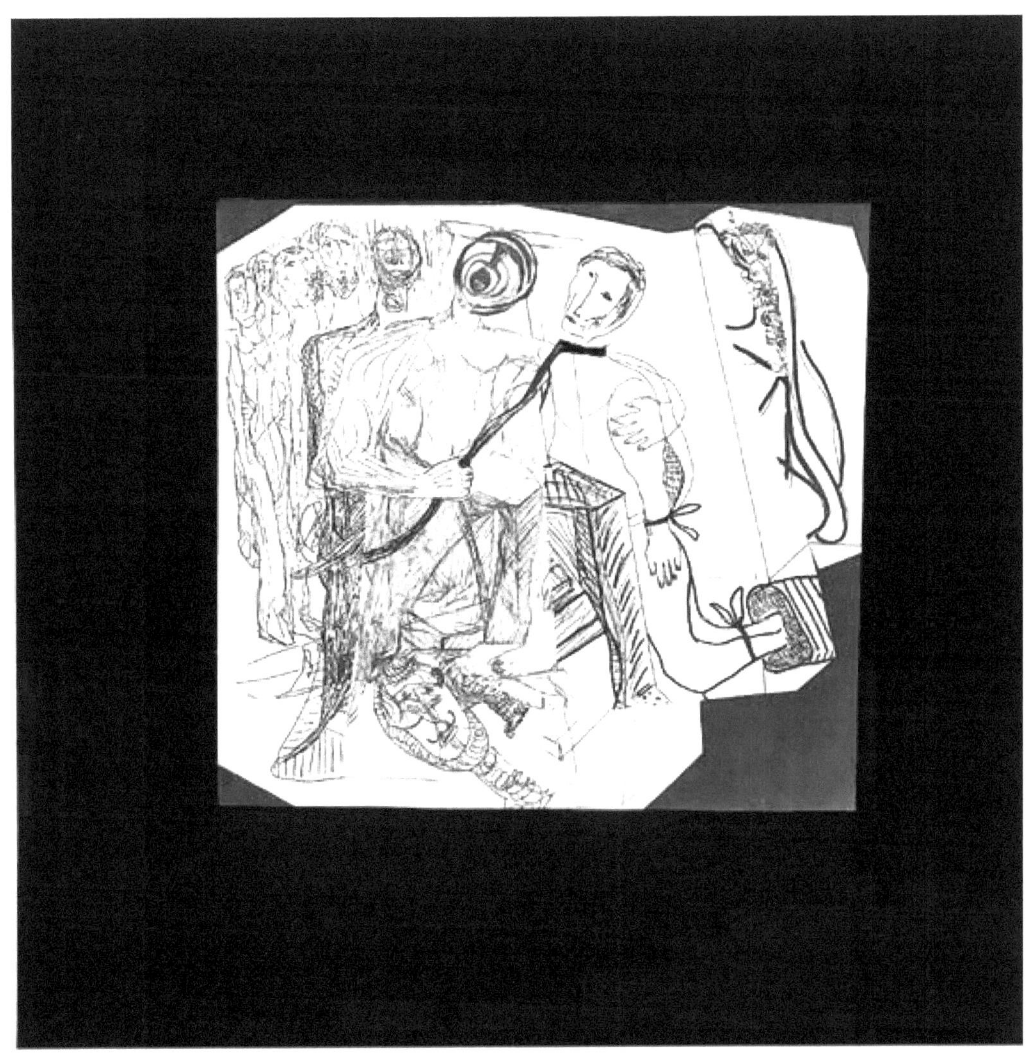

Captured intruder 6. Ink. 2023.

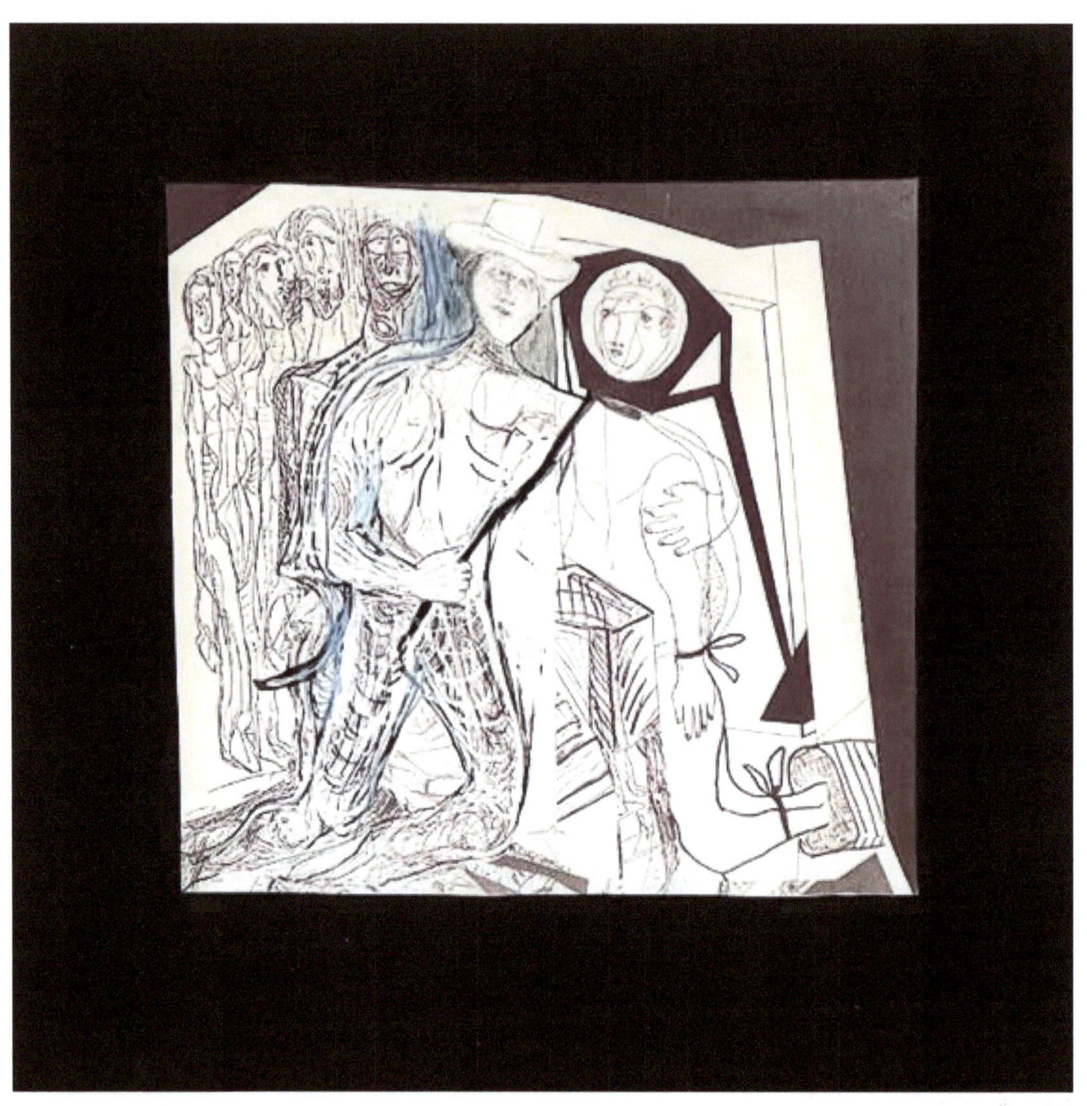

Captured intruder 7. Ink, graphite, acrylic. 2023.

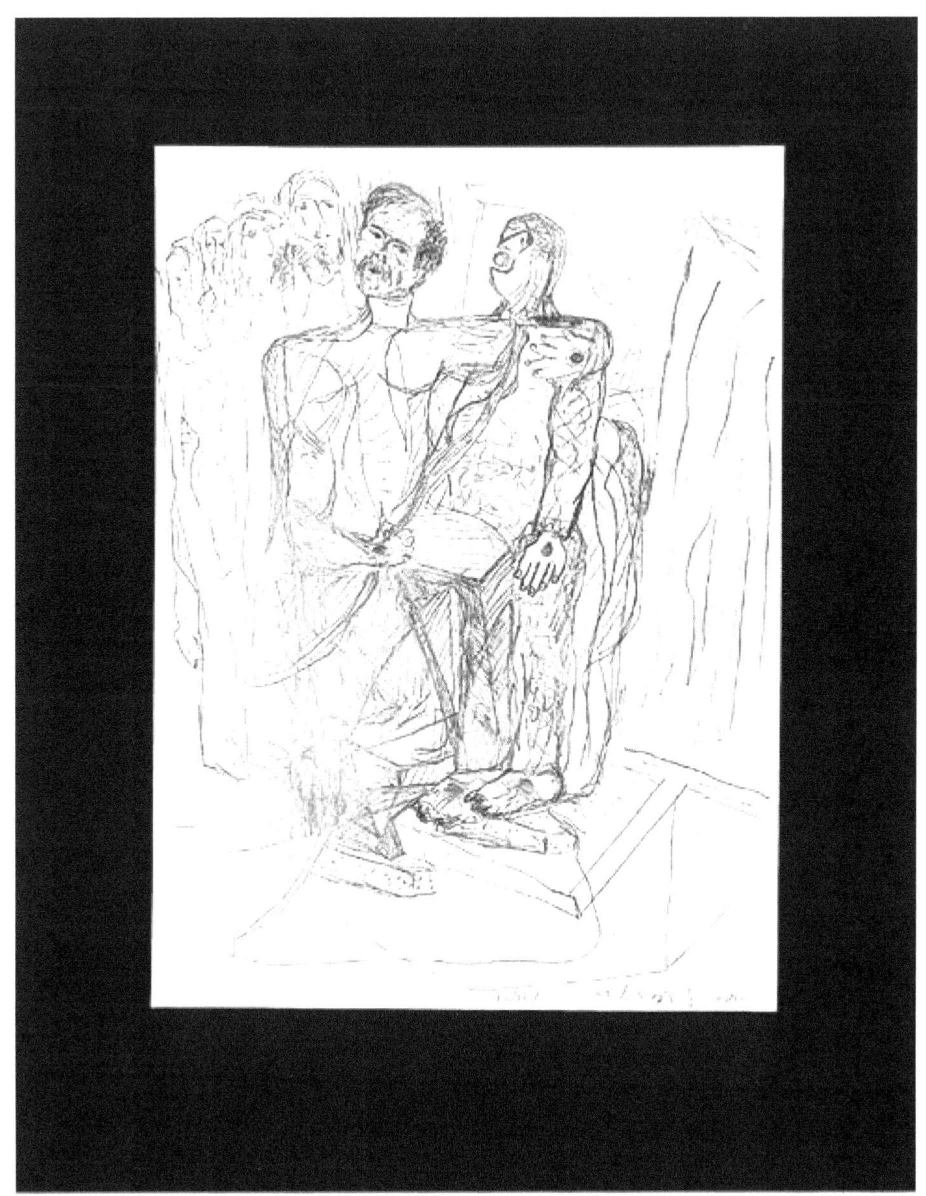

Captured intruder 8. Ink and graphite. 2023.

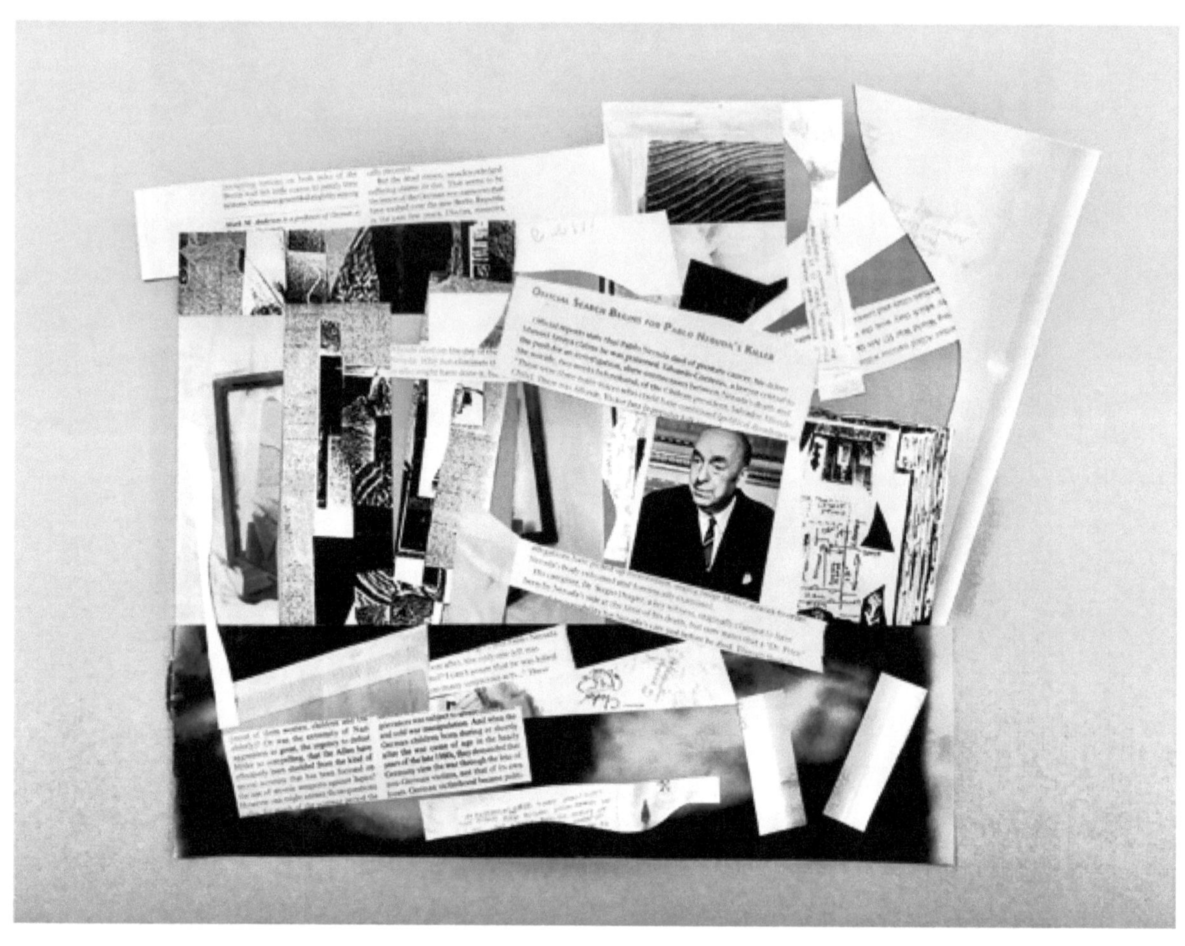

Neruda in the title. Ink, text, photomontage. 2012

The cut-up text documents Pablo Neruda's assassination through lethal injection.

I'll tell what the dead hare is in Joseph Beuys's *How to Explain Pictures to a Dead Hare* that wasn't a dead hare either to be butchered at Café La Grange, taxidermied into cigar athletic shoes Logos or auto entrapment commercials.

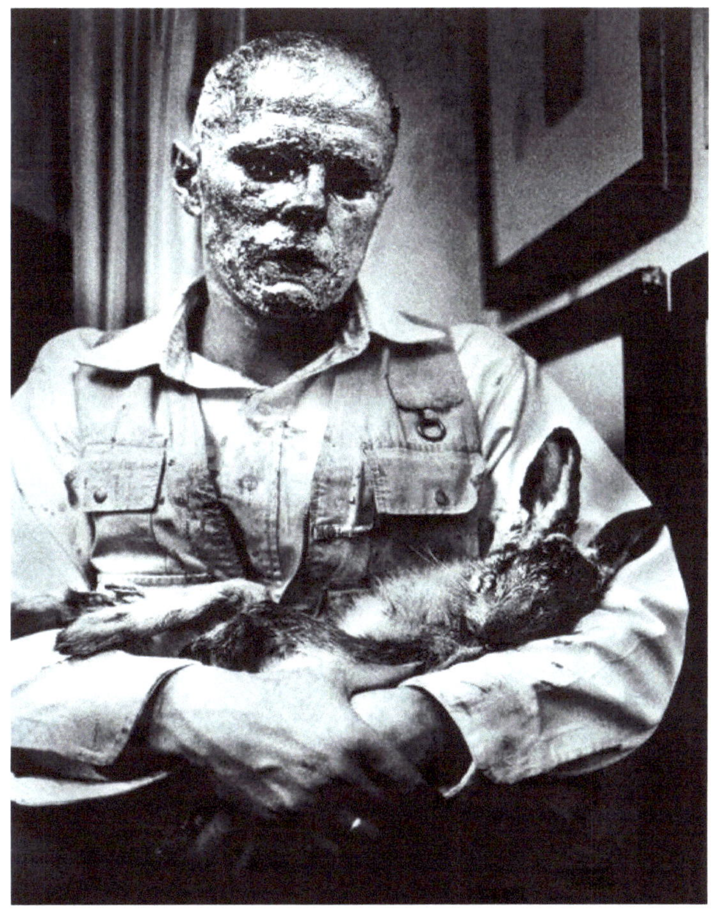

Joseph Beuys, *How to Explain Pictures to a Dead Hare* 1965

Hold on, you don't know what you're talking about explaining what a dead hare means
held in a man's arms while he explains pictures to a dead hare. This isn't some stand-up
theoretician you indulge making eccentric jokes because someone explains pictures
to a dead hare dream lever image isolated dead hare. You can't read it like some performance
idiot spectacle, after all the places they heard about a man explaining pictures to a dead hare until
they were taken away from them, so as to never have to withstand experiencing never forget
experiencing that content prohibited again, taken out of them again, until watching the man
holding a dead hare in his arms explain pictures to a dead hare to us.
The totalitarian citizen cannot forget this and does not know this.

How many times do I have to remind you? There was this man used to show up to explain
pictures to a dead hare. One time finishing his coffee he said, That coffee is strong enough to
make a snake stand up on its ass. I was always looking for this coffee.
Sometimes annotating his digressions making notes for explaining pictures to a dead hare
his habit was to smoke tobacco with hashish crumbled inside, pick up his dead hare
and go to a museum to explain pictures to a dead hare.

Don't mistake this man holding a dead hare for someone above holding a dead hare, he too
is vitiated in his own story since the myth of the man in *How to Explain Pictures to a Dead Hare*
is the fate of someone who stopped being a butcher, including in the metaphorical sense,
including when the ex-butcher gets taken in for questioning by Uni-State officer #QD519 who
was escorted from the room after starting the recording of the man holding a dead hare
explaining Karel Du Jardin's painting "Woman Milking a Red Cow." Listen, he said,
It took until the seventeenth century to paint dirt, plain farm dirt on the pads of a woman's feet
seen from behind tucked underneath her while she handles red cow udders, and the man, his
absolute distraction, this embodiment of a man possibly deranged in unfulfilled anticipations,
a type of man possibly hostile over ending up in this painting perpetually waiting for milk
or fingers and udders symbolic of something else latent in space, the latent
untitled unanswerable message and what brought this out of him.

After the wildfires dead hares piled up.
I'm both paranoid and pregnatoid. I always was. Why shouldn't I have been?
Who isn't someone hasn't been at the same time needing pictures explained to him
(to her)? Not this time around. Not in the same person. Not in this here U.S. chemical

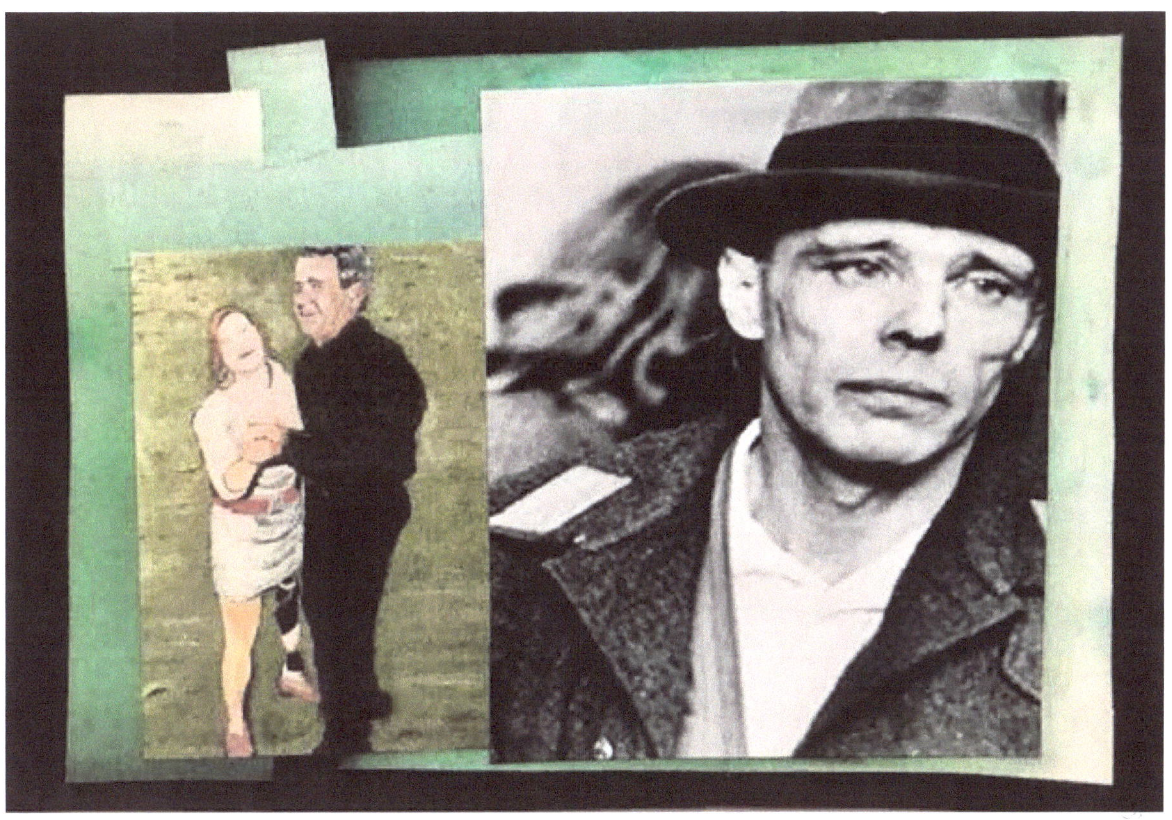

In a tail gunner's coat Explaining Bush's picture with U.S.-Iraq War Veteran amputee. Photomontage, cut-outs. 2017.

receptacle site about a mile past the Neon High Heel Motel. The Hollywood Wolfman had better luck with improvised Gypsies than the man explaining pictures to a dead hare had with candidates, incumbents, mercenaries, posses, armed villagers, police dogs, up to the volunteer armed civilian enforcements on either side.

The one explanation I don't accept in *How to Explain Pictures to a Dead Hare* is the honey and gold leaf head and facemask contained fertility symbolism, because of the creativity of bees. This here is a dead hare held in a man's arms. He is a Veteran wounded and returned to battle five times. Maybe he used to be a male bulimic or he's a peyote shaman. Or. Or.

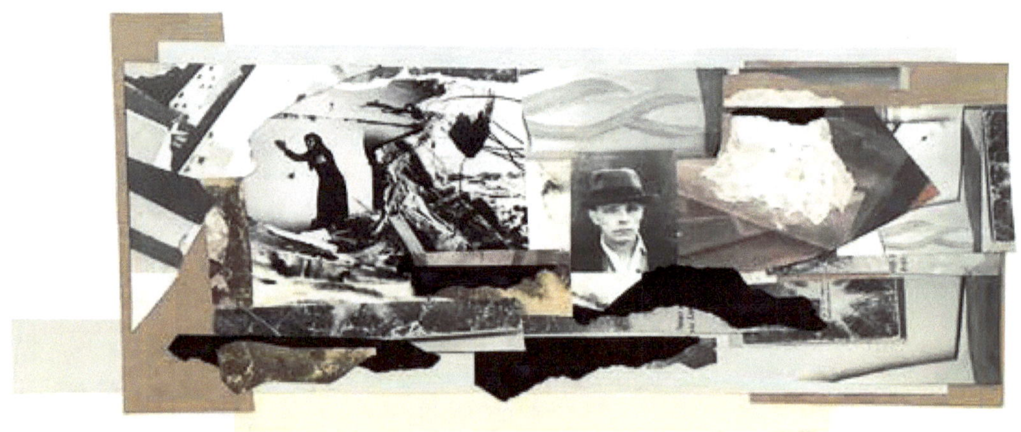

Joseph Beuys explains Palestine to Lorca's remains. Photomontage. 2017.

Who knows what else happened to him before he started explaining pictures to a dead hare.

He explains pictures to himself to understand how to explain pictures to a dead hare.
He has a honey and gold leaf head and face mask because he is a clown.
Only a clown with honey and gold leaf covering his head could talk with a straight face
to a dead hare. The fact is the honey and gold leaf hurt the clown's head. In sequences.
And then redundantly.

The last time he was a dead hare the museums were shut down, a dead hare fed him plain onion broth with soy enzymes. Something contested as favorable to be remembered existed as honey and gold leaf. Something erased existed as a dead hare.

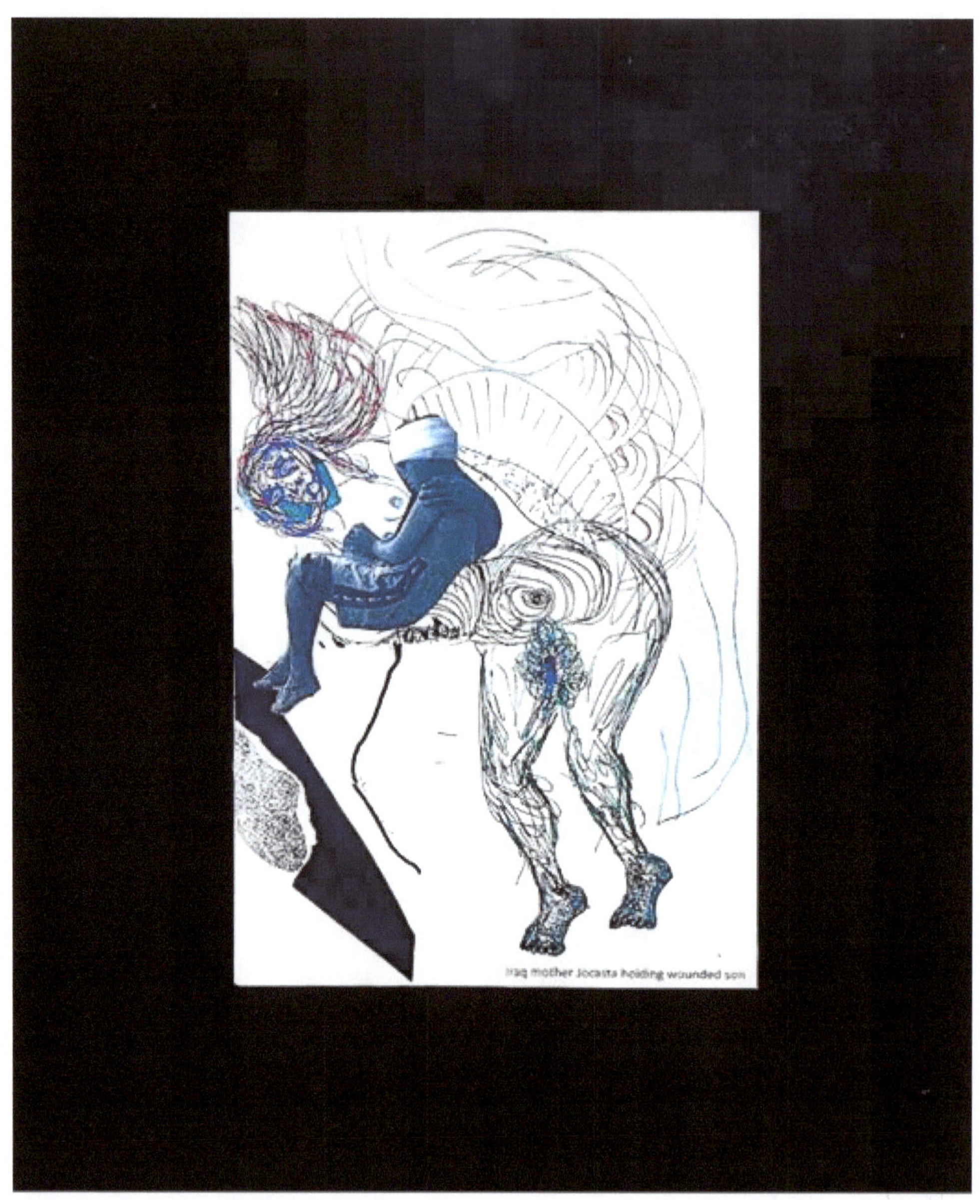

Palestinian mother explains Israel to her wounded son. Ink and photomontage. 2003, 2016.

Introspection Sequence Two

Recovered From

There's a naïve exhilarance to a person writing down a dream.
The manner he felt less subtracted.
Wait, wait a second, I dreamed I was an infant dreaming.
What did I know, all I knew, the one thing I clung to,
the reprieves coming my way, I wasn't even aware I needed them,
I didn't see a reception, I can't explain favoritism, I don't understand
the whim of procedure at all.
I estimated the weight. I observed a fantasy of the sexes,
the color gradations, separate leg lengths, how the designs
were arranged, the patterns, the hyper-luminous differential
rose gray day moths forcing down a Oaxaca sage petal.
The floating pollen table.
Driven to where they were going.
Close as I'll get to nature today.
Close as I'll get to the rose gray ardent grain.
I dreamed I was an infant dreaming.
Close as I'll get to a breast or shoulder today.
Had all the time I needed. One time.
I struggled. I raised my fists against something,
a curtain, a crow's shadow, Plumbago without blossoms,
ragged twine. Then relaxed my arms, then relaxed my fat, my
entire face squinted in privacy, using a sort of breast of my left
hand as a sort of pillow.

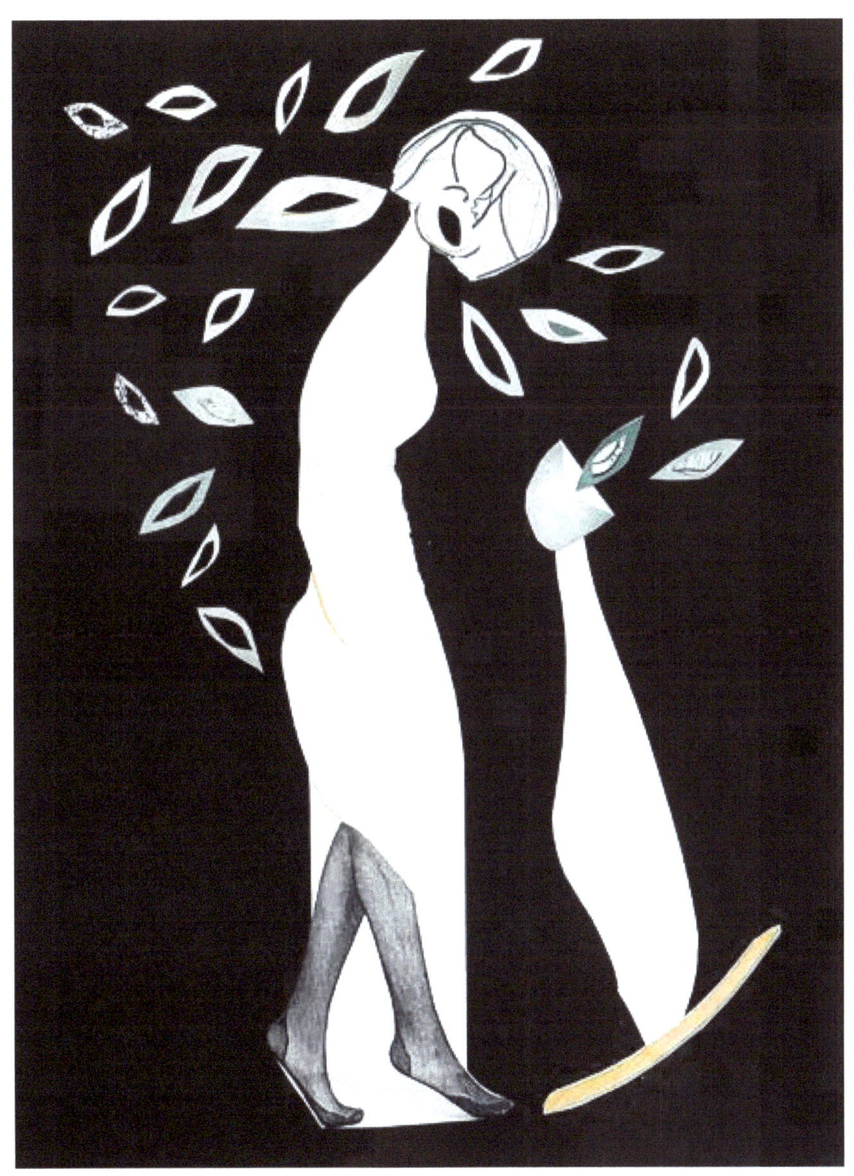

Producer. Ink, cut-out, photomontage. 2023.

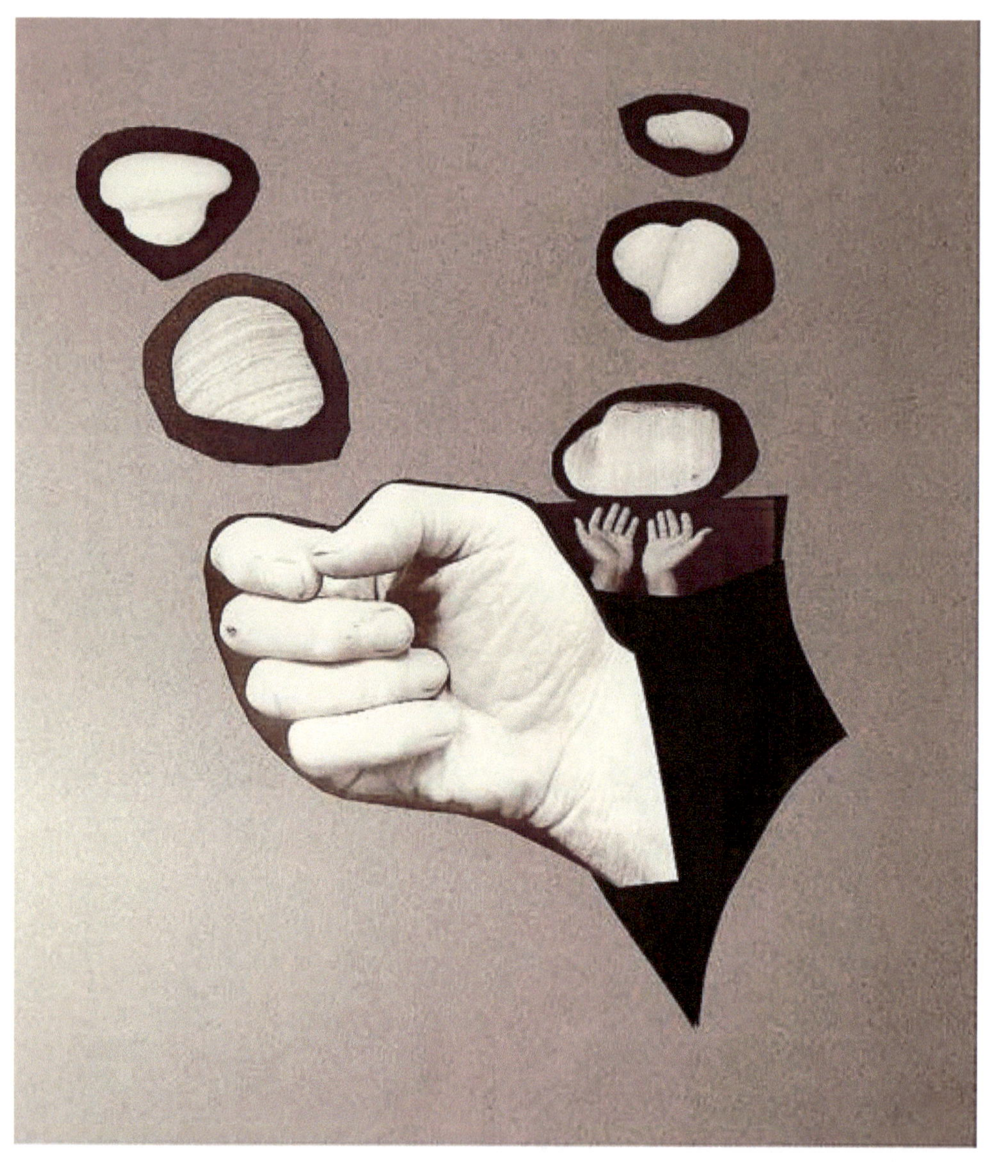

Farewell Jerome Rothenberg, Neeli Cherkovski, Marjorie Perloff, friends of the imagination that matters. Photomontage. 2024.

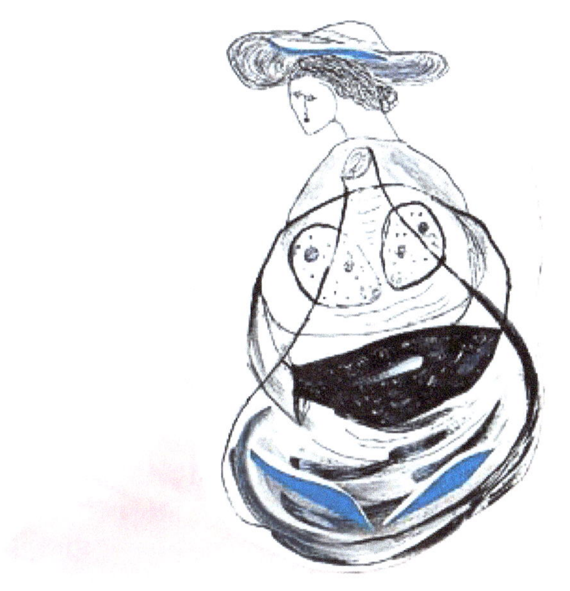

Unconscious Gift Machine. Ovulator. Ink and watercolor. 2021.

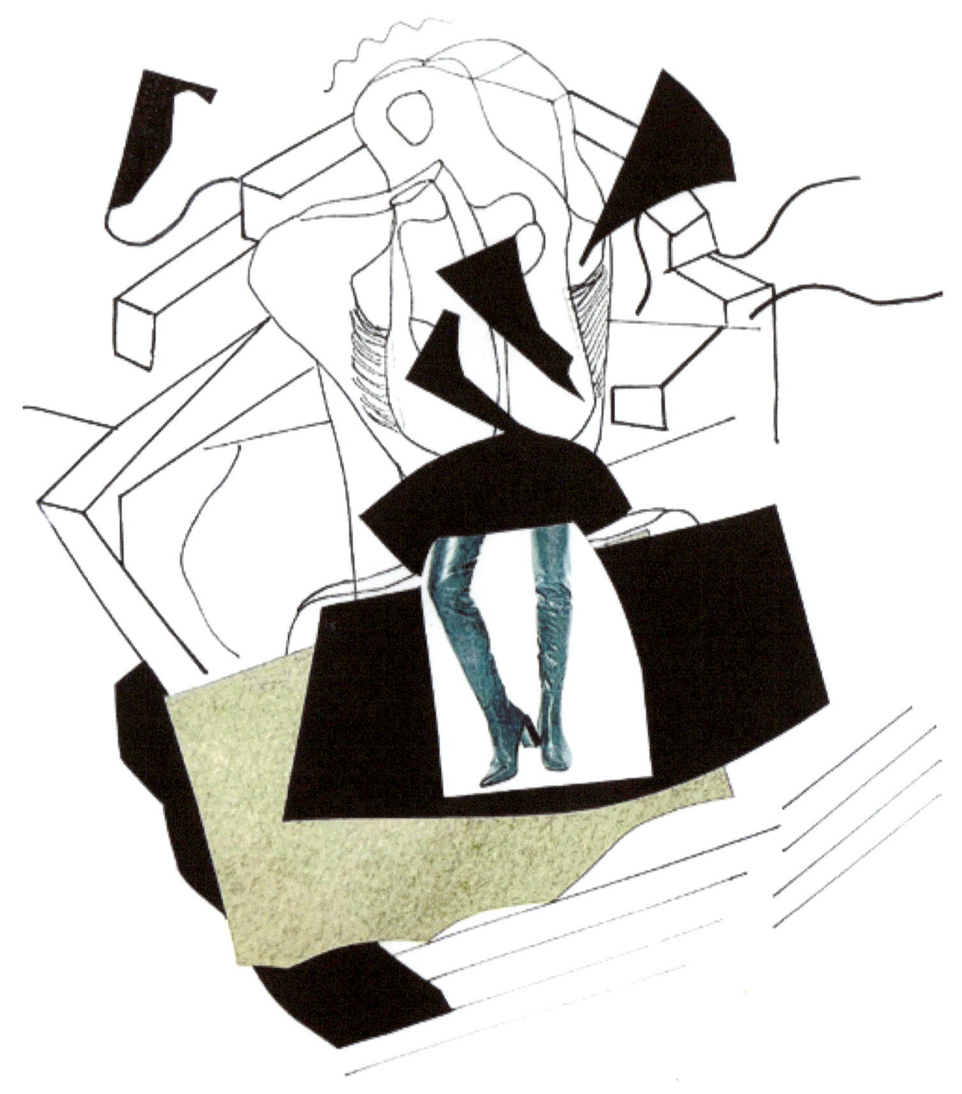

Unconscious Gift Machine. Visitor. Ink and cut-outs. 2021.

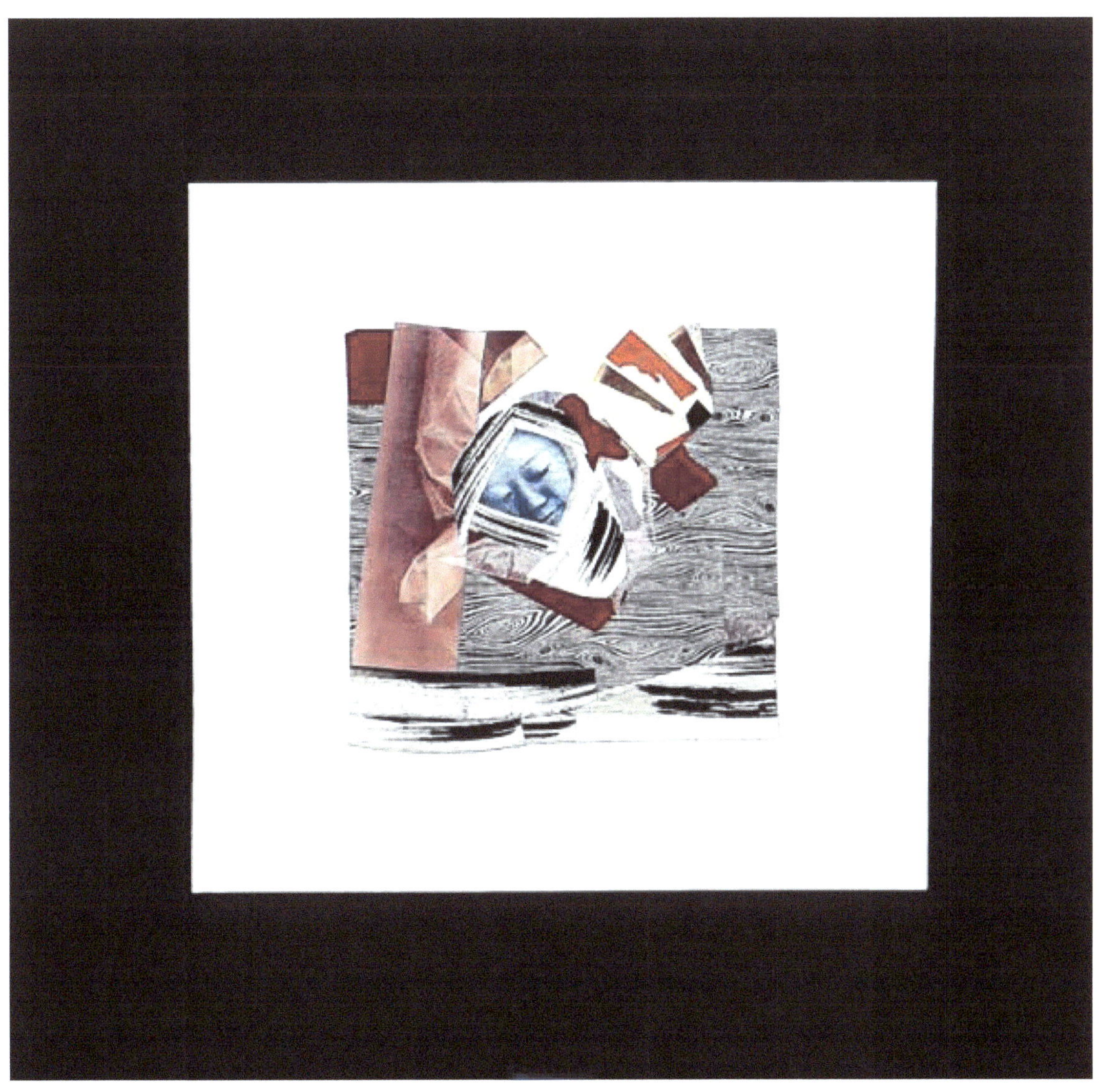

All the characters in my life are dreaming. Ink and photomontage. 2010, 2023.

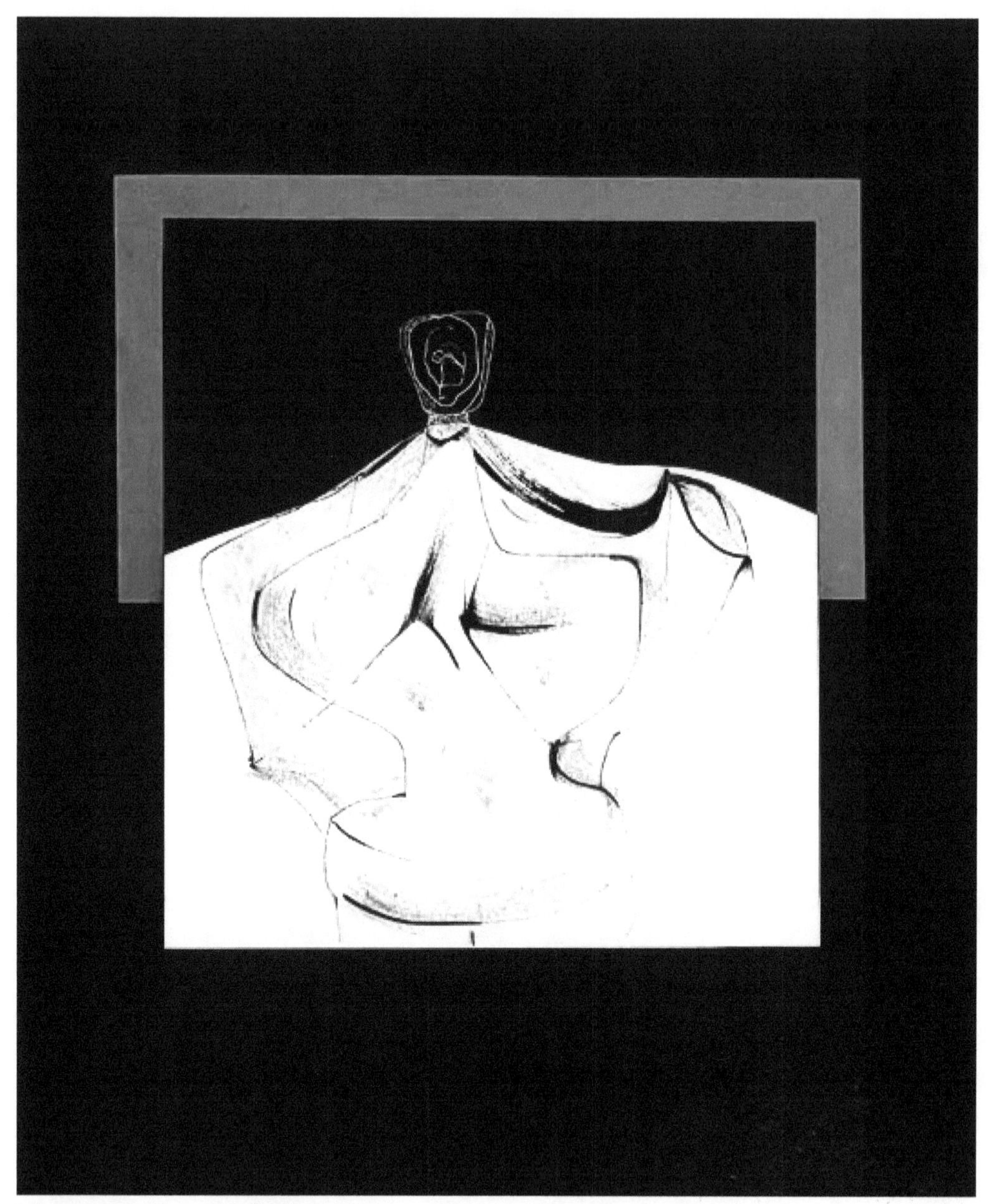

Unconscious Gift Machine. Heritage. Ink and cut-outs. 2022.

Erotic Feelings Two

The Pigeon Ritual

You have to remember we were just bodies attached to hair.
Birds of hair, wings and nests of hair.
Our beards sideburns armpits were sexual contraptions.
It was a sexual epidemic.
The woman he later depended on immediately recognized his beard.
They had what we called The Pigeon Ritual.
She let him see the purple dot under her wing,
He raised his leg to let her know.
Third, fourth week, in April, after the first thaw.
Up there anyway. As it all begins. The heat palpable.
The yearning going both ways. Their tongues lapping back
then forth, then backwards continuing forthwards.
After yearning, after fatigue, their agitated excitement,
they poked and snapped at each other with their beaks.
They beat each other a little with their wings.
They traded off cleaning each other.
They did what they did. You, you say you don't,
but you remember The Pigeon Ritual.

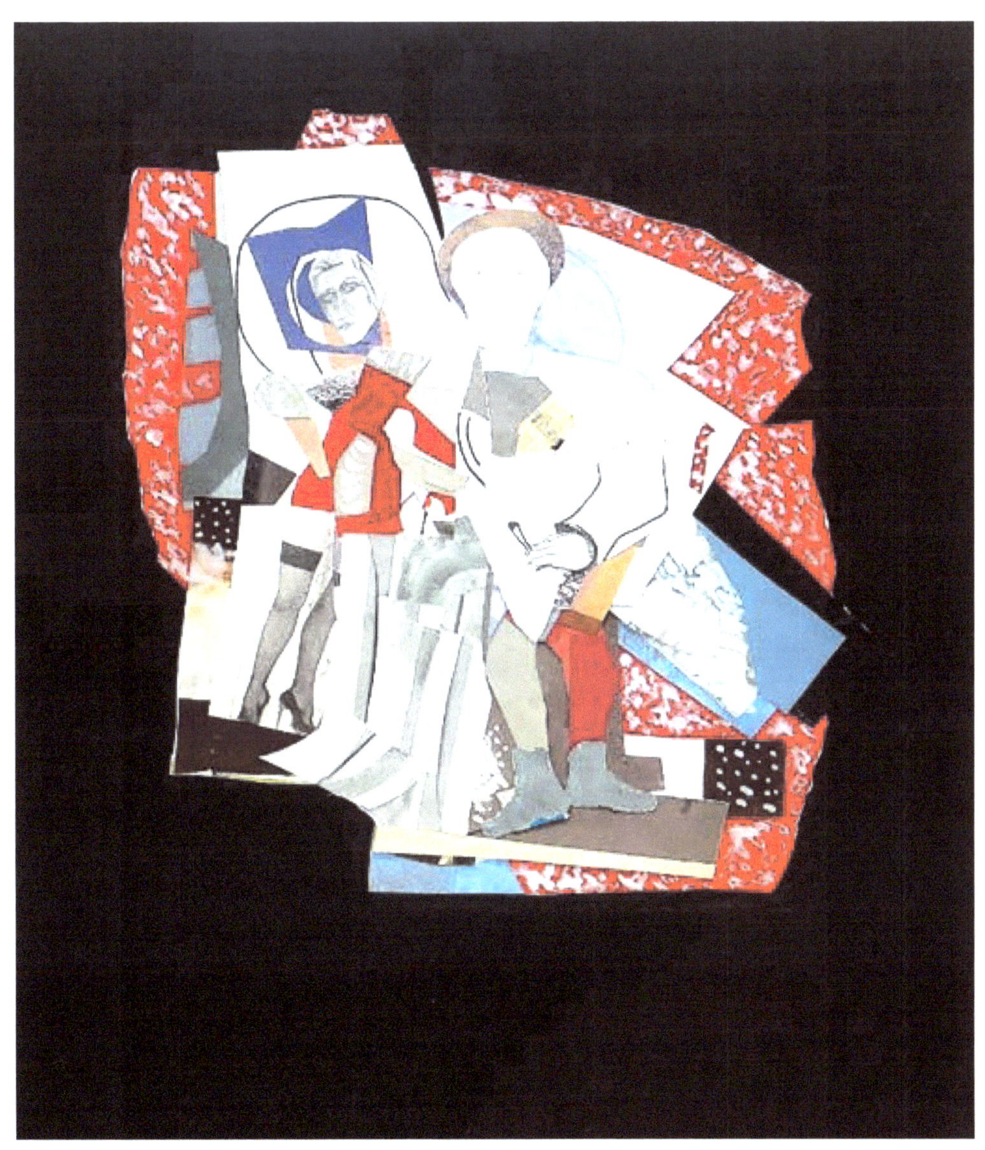

Experimental couple. Ink, graphite, cut-outs, acrylic. 2017, 2024.

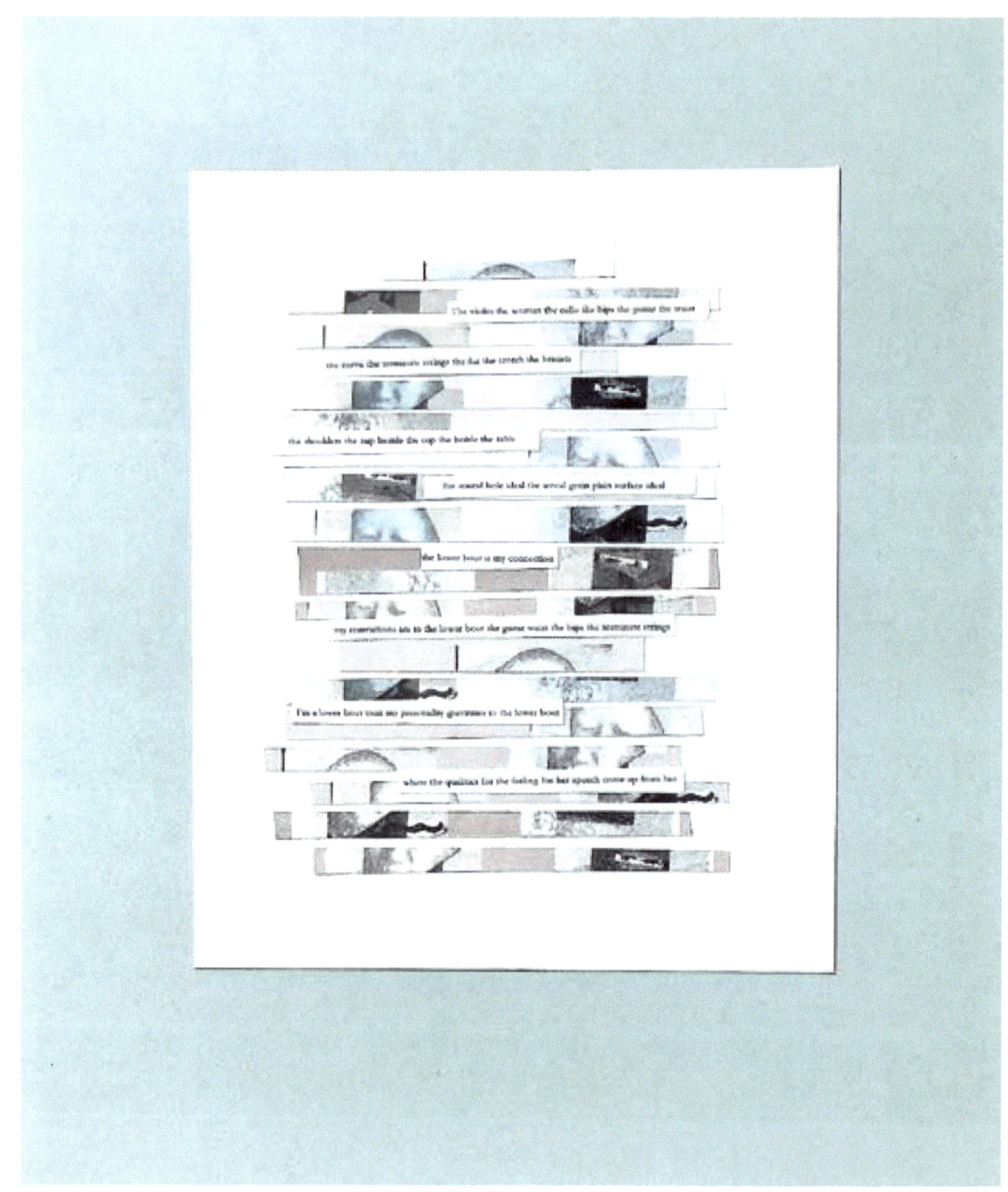

Gravitates. Poem and photomontage. 2014.

Gravitates

the violin the woman the cello the hips the guitar the waist
the curve the terminate strings the fur the crotch the breasts
the shoulders the cup beside the cup the bottle the table
the sound hole ideal the wood grain plain surface ideal
the lower bout is my connection
my convictions are to the lower bout the guitar waist the hips the terminate strings
I'm a lower bout man my personality gravitates to the lower bout
where the qualities for the feeling for her speech come up from

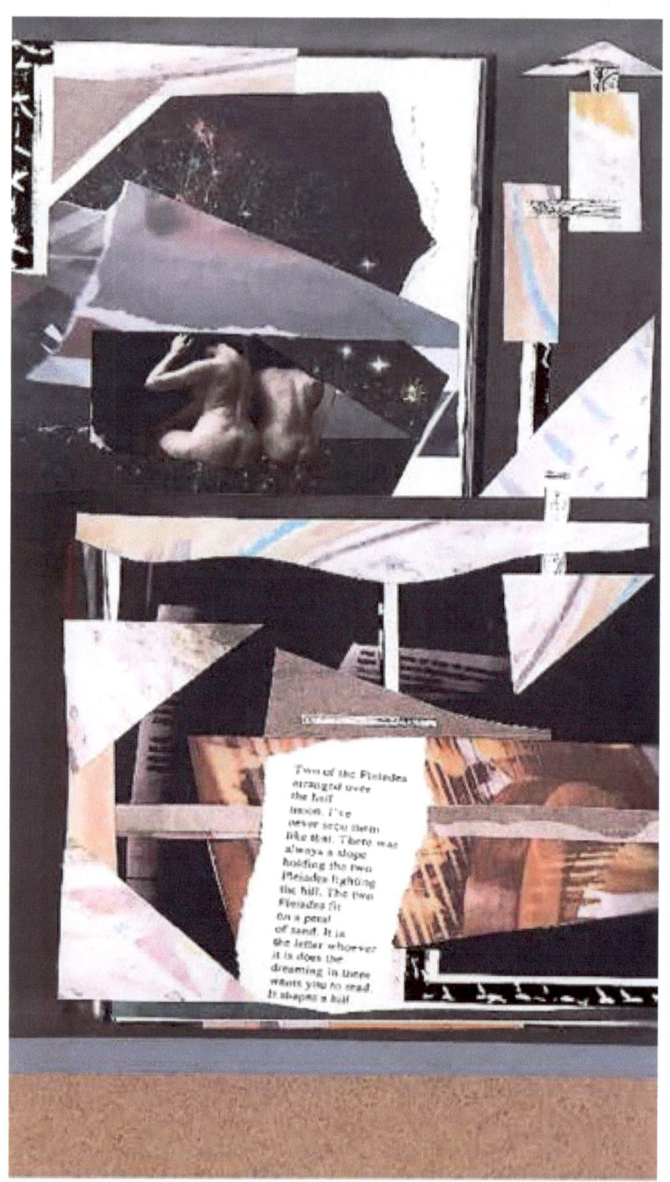

Two of the Pleiades. Poem and photo montage. 2014.

Two of the Pleiades

arranged over
the half
moon. I've
never seen them
like that. there was
always a slope
holding the two
Pleiades lighting
the hill. The two
Pleiades fit
on a petal
of sand. It is
the letter whoever
it is does the
dreaming in there
wants you to read.
It shapes a hill.

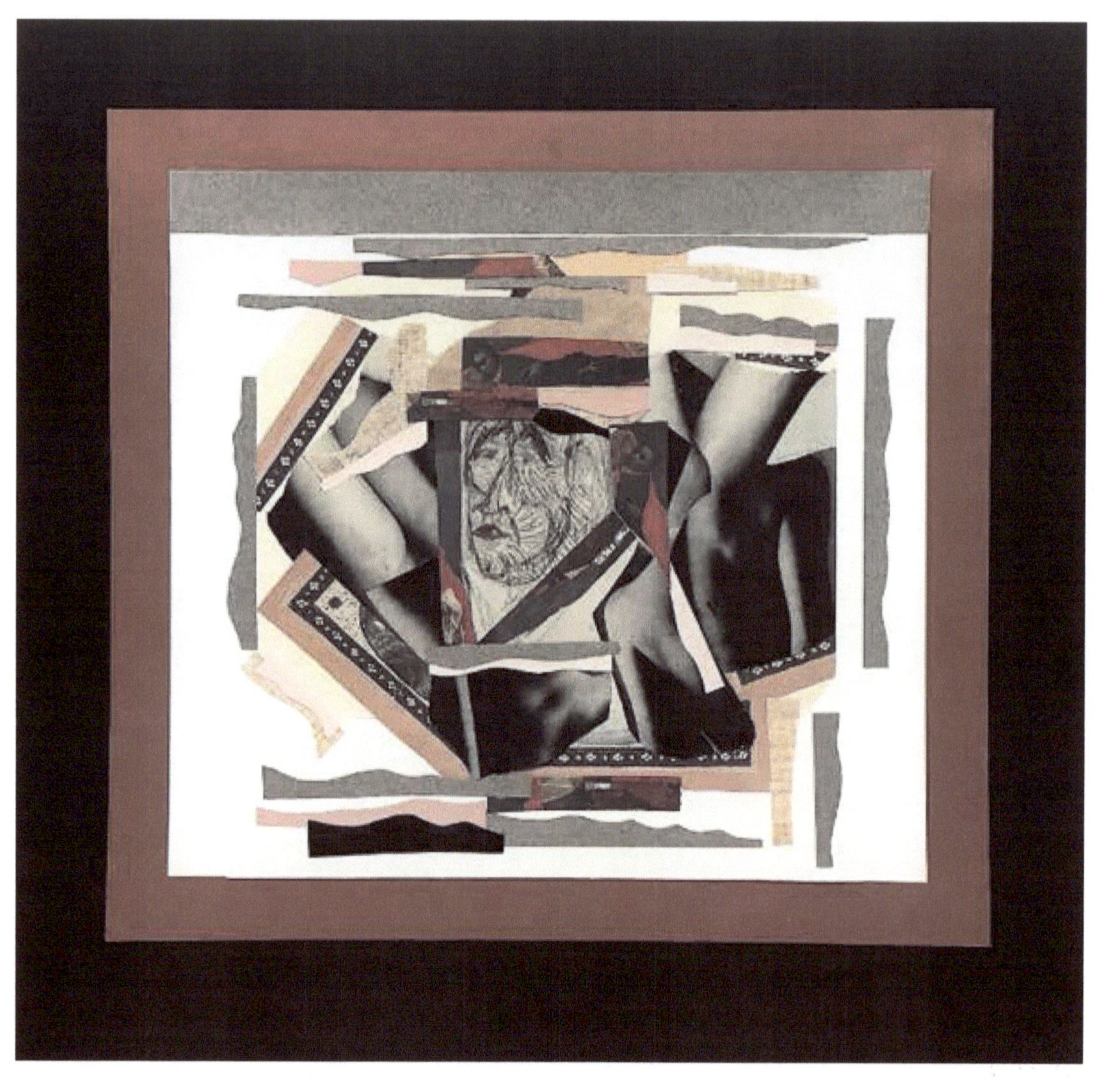

Erotic love introspected. Photomontage, ink, cut-outs. 2001, 2016.

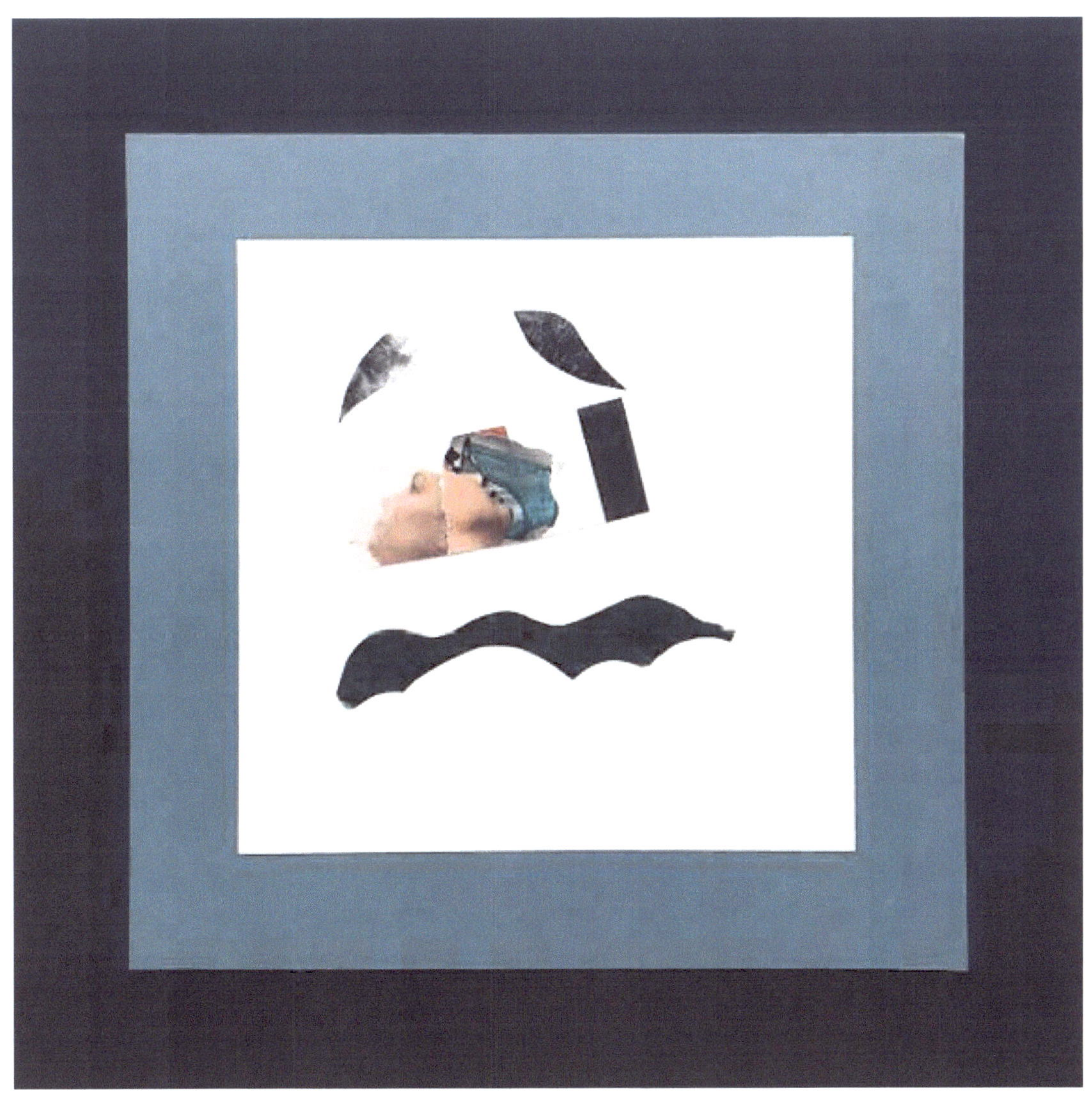

Introspecter. Photomontage and cut-outs. 2014.

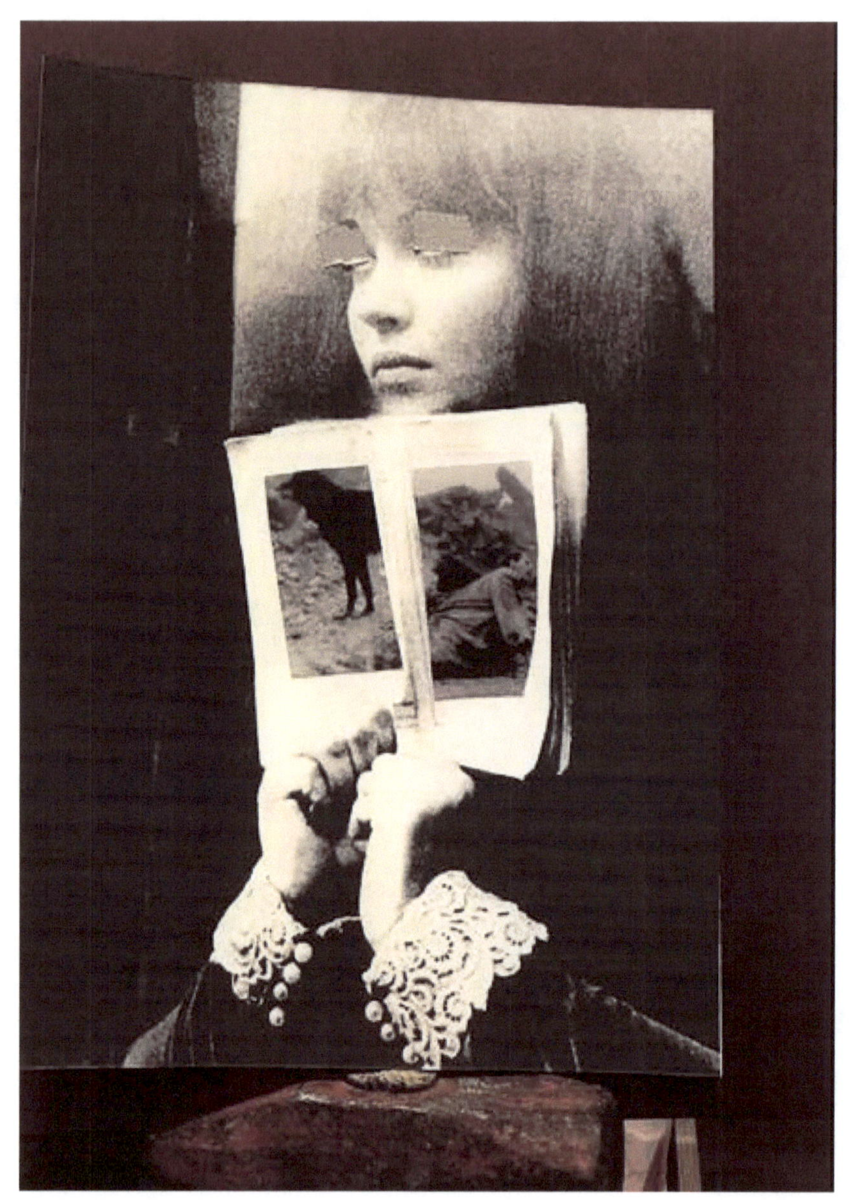

Three-character noir. Photomontage, cross peen hammer head. 2017.

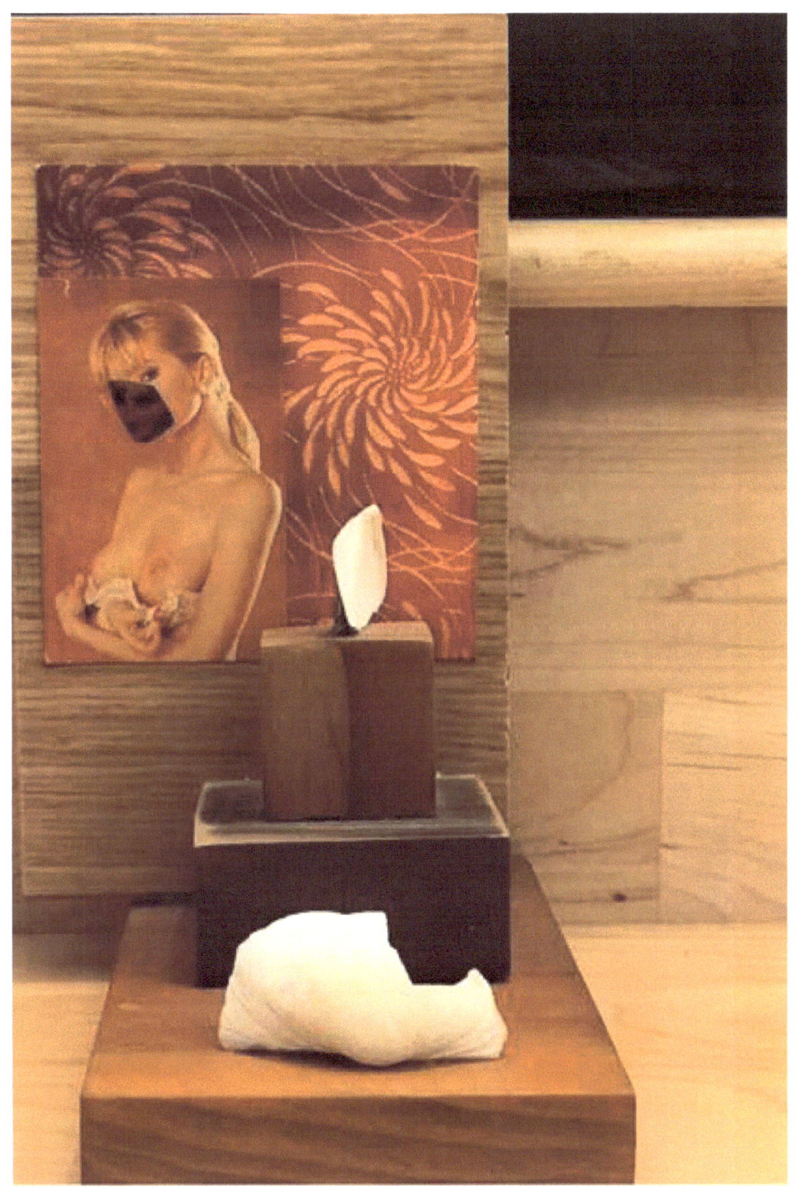

Visit, riser. Mixed media and photomontage.1998, 2013.

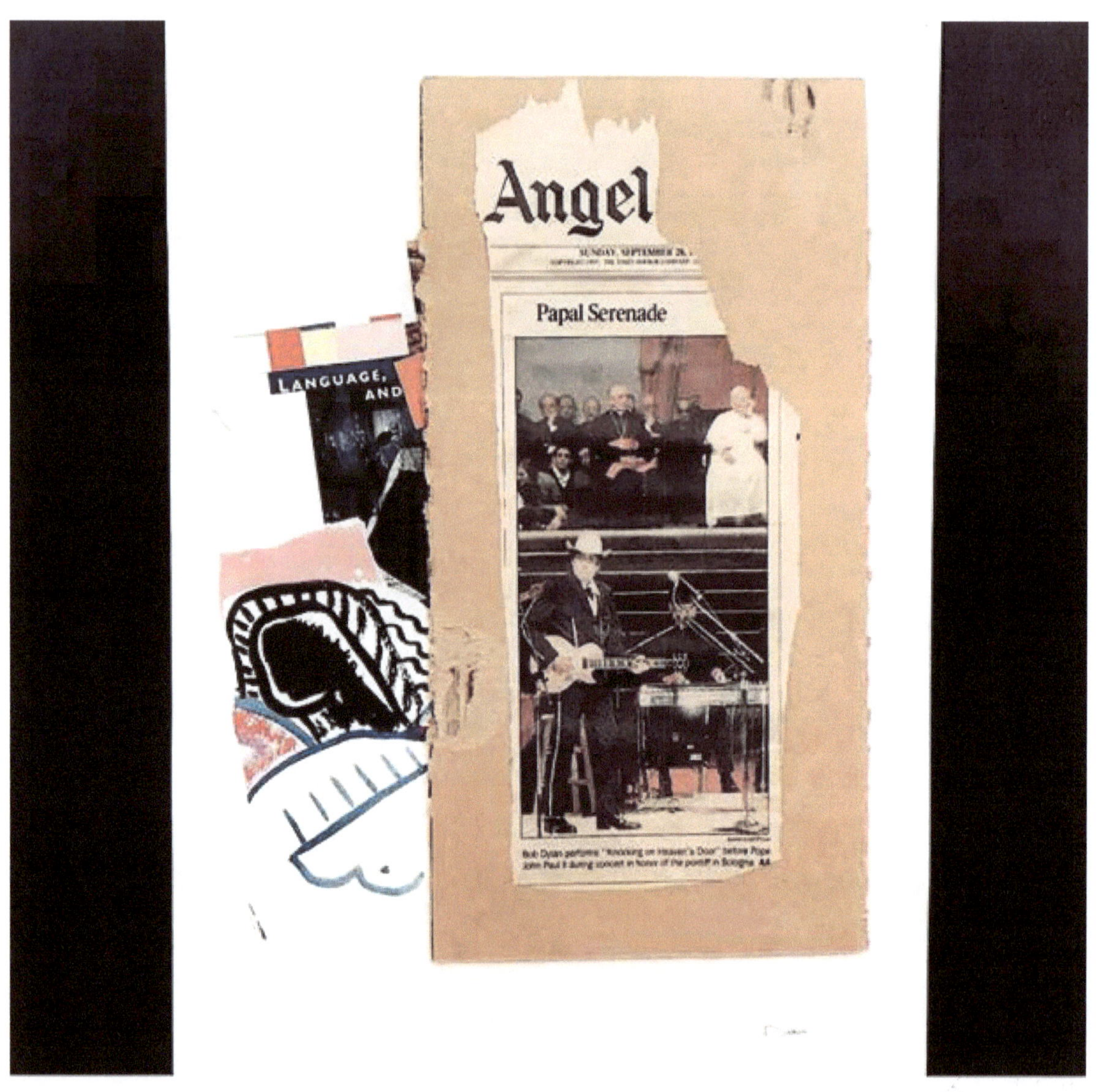

Complicated muse. Watercolor, text, photomontage. 1986, 1997, 2008.

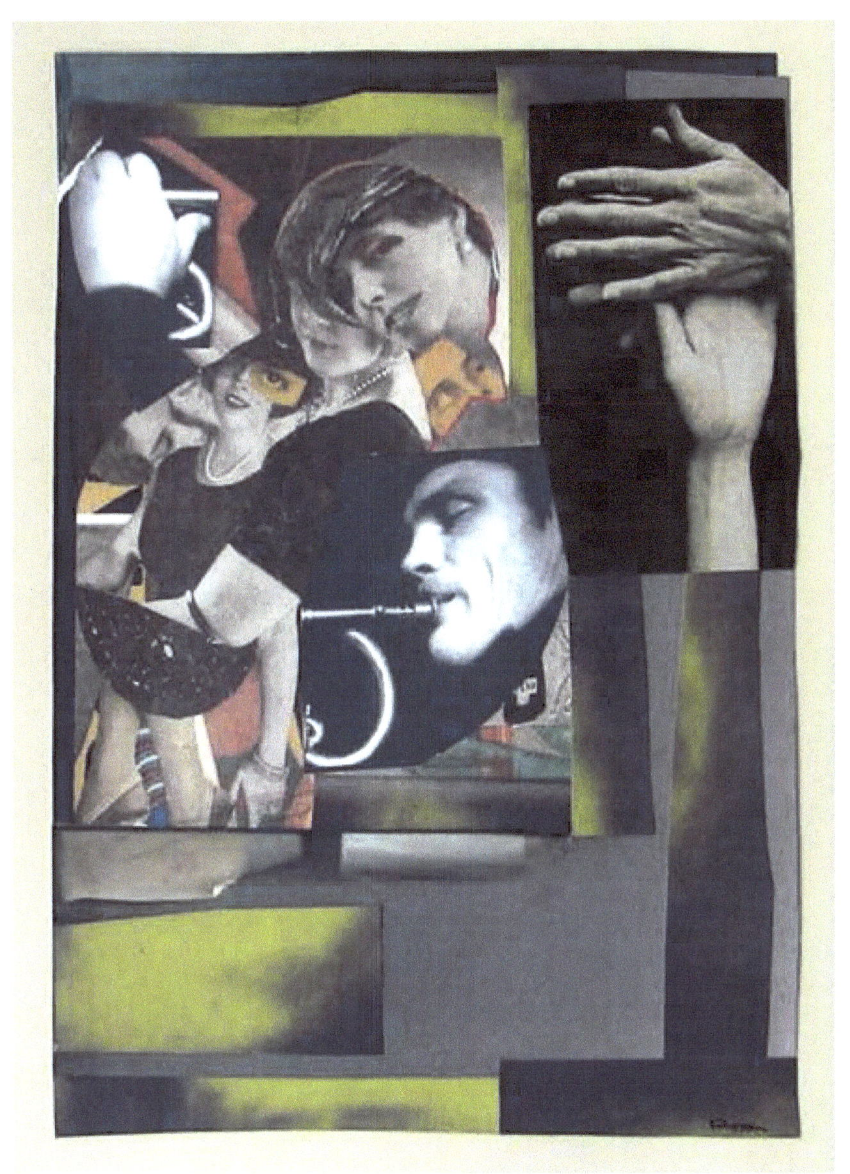

Hanna und Chet. Photomontage and cut-outs. 2014.

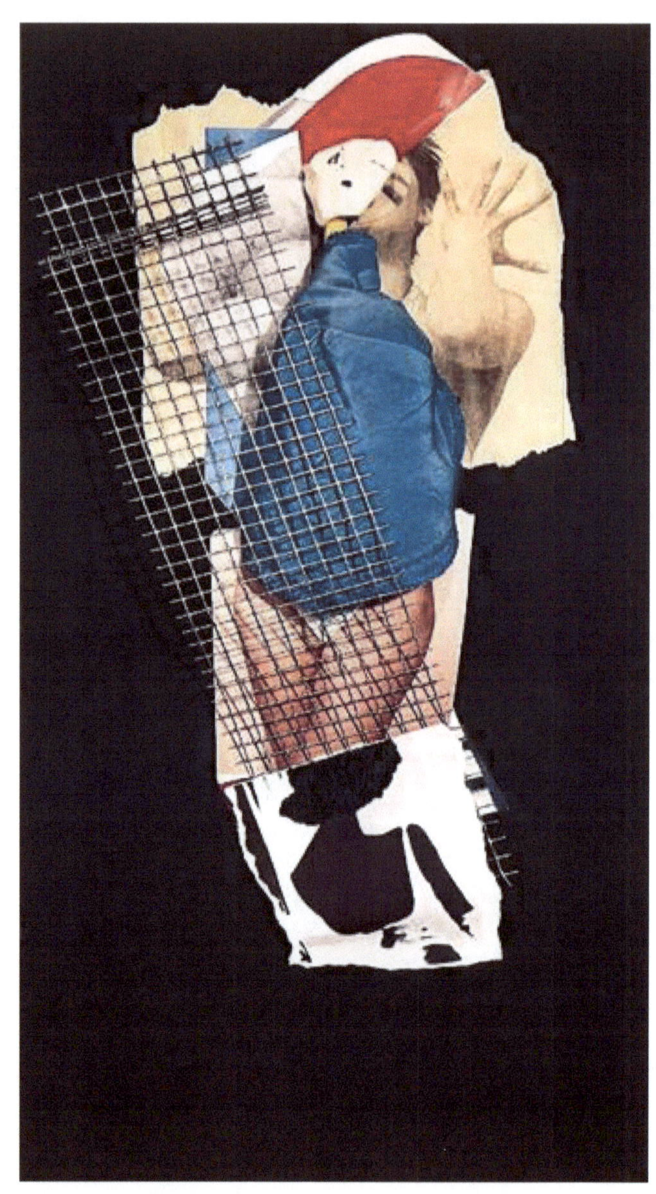

Hostage libido. Photomontage, cloth, shell, wire. 1999, 2012, 2022.

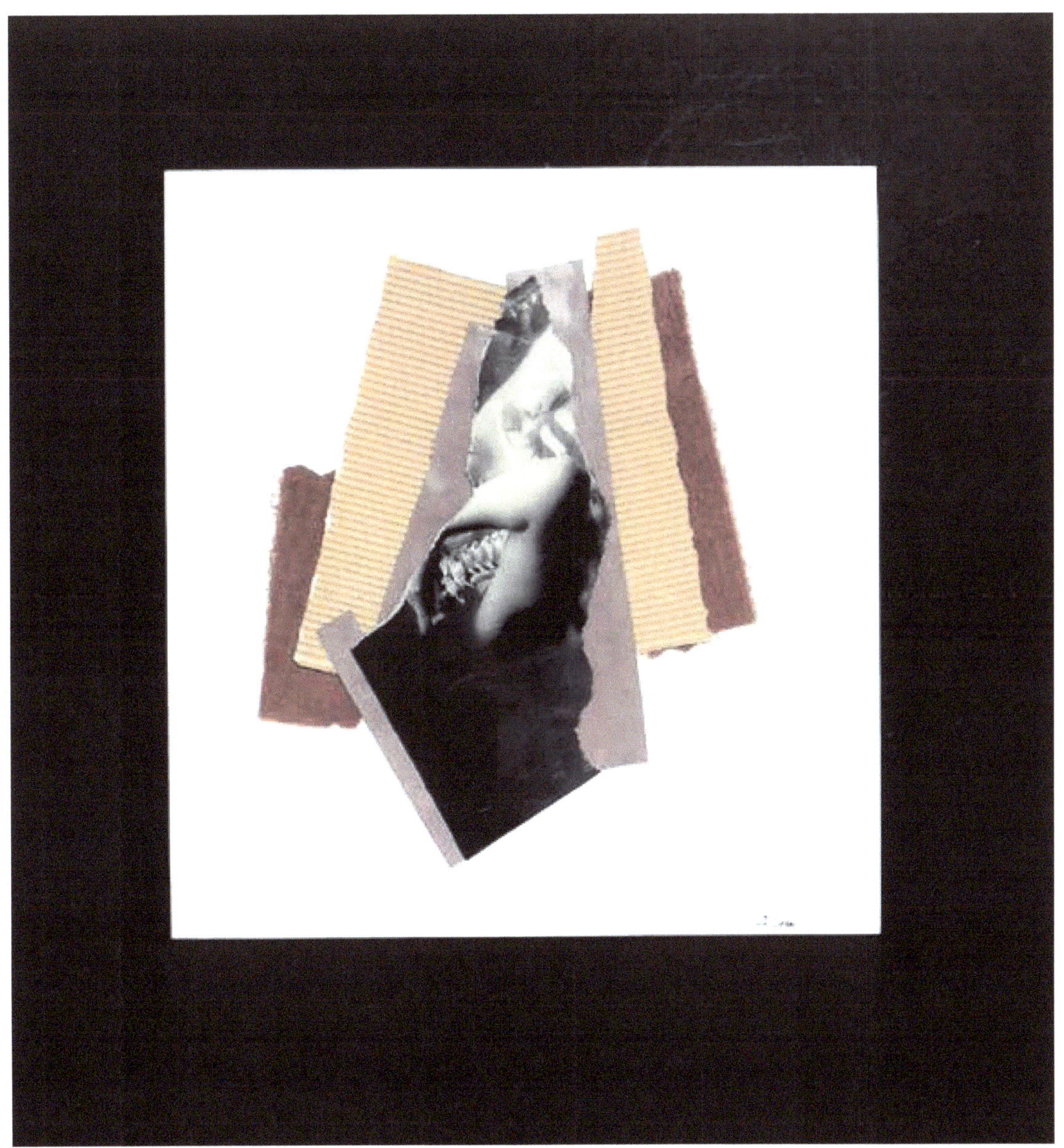

Feminine 3. Photomontage, cloth, paper. 1999.

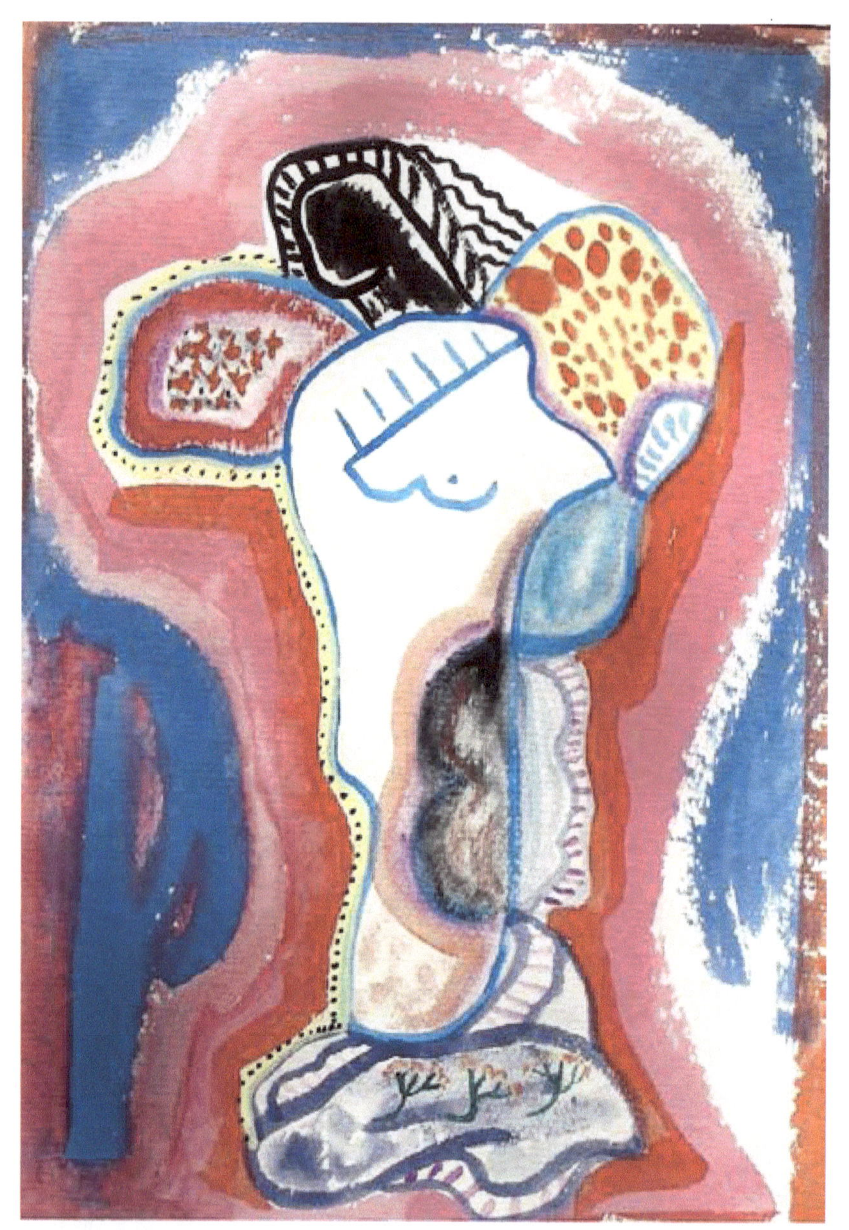

Muse on Crete. Watercolor. 1987.

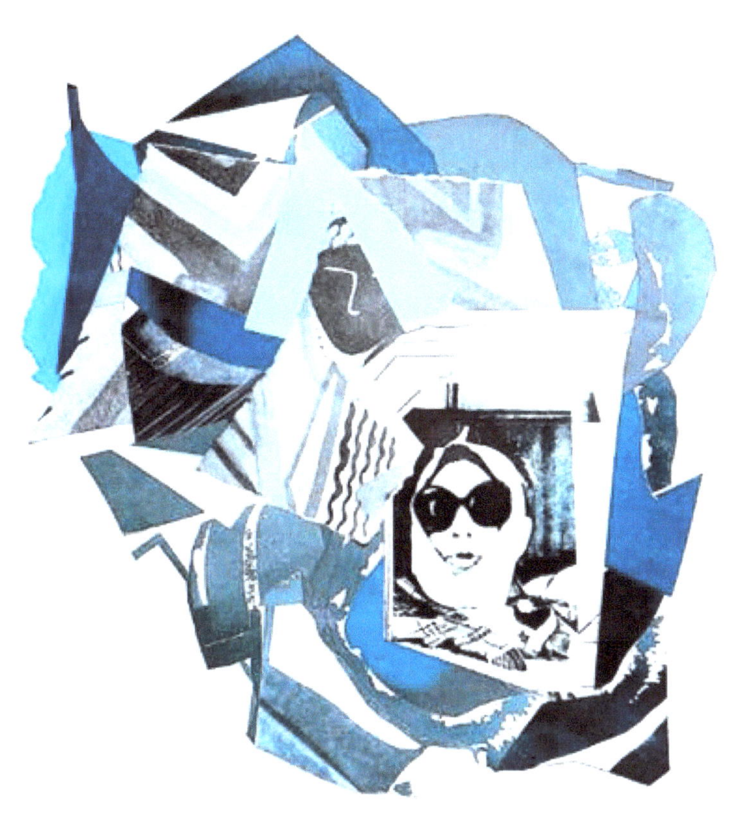

LJ itinerary.Watercolor, ink, cut out, photomontage. 2017, 2021.

List of Works

Sympathetic Manifesto: Selected Poems, 1975-2015.
Apocalypse Contemporary (on Sharon Doubiago's work). 2019.
Twin Extra. 2015.
Title to Pussy Riot. 2014.
Amnesty Muse. 2011.
My Piece of the Puzzle. Awarded the Josephine Miles PEN Award in Poetry, 2008.
Parking Lot Mood Swing: Autobiographical Monologues and Prose Poetry. 2004.
Driving Face Down. 2001. Awarded The Blue Lynx Prize in Poetry, 2001.
The Donkey's Tale. 1998.
*Double Muse.*1997.
Dignity in Naples and North Hollywood, introduction by Philip Levine, 1996.
Two Poems. 1995.
*Under the Black Moth's Wings.*1987.
Sympathetic Manifesto. 1986.
Seduction of the Groom. 1982.
The Roots and the Towers. 1980.
Detonated Veils. 1976.

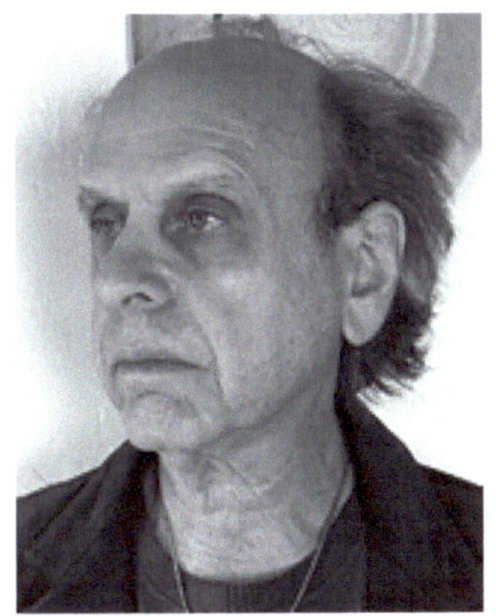

Doren Robbins' writing has appeared in many periodicals, including *Kayak, Sulfur, The American Poetry Review, New Letters, The Iowa Review, Lana Turner* and *Salt.* His current book, *Sympathetic Manifesto, Selected Poems 1975-2015* was published in 2021 (Spuyten Duyvil Press) is out of print. There are a few copies available from the author at robbinsdoren@fhda.edu. As a poet and artist, Robbins organized readings and produced posters to benefit The Romero Relief Fund and The Salvadoran Medical Relief Fund during the Salvadoran Civil War; and for poetsagainst-thewar.com at the beginning of the American-Iraq-Afghanistan Wars. He taught literature and creative writing at Foothill College, 2001-2022.

Acknowledgements

Agave: "Unconscious Gift Machine Ovulator." (magazine cover).
Angryoldman: John Cassavetes observes.
Another Chicago Magazine: "Black nephew archetype."
Artemis: "Itinerant Dreamer."
Caliban.com: "Migraine noir."
Catamaran: "Gravitates" and "Two of the Pleiades."
Cholla Needles: "Complicated muse."
Club Plum: "Introspection" and "Mother of permanently disabled Vet mirror."
Insurgent Imagination: "Untitled Backstory."
Lana Turner: "I'll tell what the dead hare is in Joseph Beuys's *How to Explain Pictures to a Dead Hare.*"
militanthumanist.org: "Captured intruder 1-6."
The Sparring Artists: Literary Anthology of Sparring with Beatnik Ghosts: "Farewell Neeli Cherkovski, Marjorie Perloff, Jerome Rothenberg, friends of the consciousness that matters," and "Captured Invader 3."
The Ontological Museum, New Acquisitions 2019: "Visitor."
Otoliths: "The Iron Heel Sequence 1-5." "Iraq mother Jocasta." "Boundary in the Title."
Paterson Museum of Art: "Muse on Crete" (writers' that are artists group exhibition).
Red Wheelbarrow: "Hostage libido" and "Title in the image."
Third Rail: "Rexroth to him now."
Twin Extra: "Hanna und Chet" (book cover).
Utriculi: "Copulating shopping carts," "Shopping cart tossed into LACMA tar pit," "Shopping cart action figure," "Shopping cart femininity," "Recycled shopping carts supported by right foot."
Monologue Poem: "Under the world's Leadership there's a lot of shopping carts."

Poems

"Jewdog." *Driving Face Down.* Lynx House Press. 2001.
"The Sexiest Part." *Amnesty Muse.* Wild Horse Press. 2011.
"Recovered from" and "The Pigeon Ritual" appeared in *Milk: A Poetry Magazine.* Number 4/5. 2015.
"Joseph Beuys, How to Explain Pictures to a Dead Hare 1965" appeared in Lana Turner 14. 2021.

www.ingramcontent.com/pod-product-compliance
Lightning Source LLC
LaVergne TN
LVHW070124110826
845147LV00002B/185

* 9 7 9 8 9 9 2 4 5 8 2 1 3 *